Praise for *The Missing Peace*

"This book is an intimate and inspiring glimpse into one woman's journey from turbulence to peace, from chaos to calm. A generous offering to any reader wondering how to shift from surviving to thriving."

—Jan Phillips, author, *Still On Fire*

"Nere has a contagious enthusiasm for choosing peace as our highest aspiration. She shows us that living a peace-filled life starts with the intention to do so and with each page we can feel her longing to inspire us to pivot toward peace, no matter what. 'It's a choice,' she says, offering us plenty of tips to get started on our journey. She uses stories from her own long and diverse life, such that we can feel how the journey to peace unfolded for her and can imagine the same for ourselves. She encourages us to investigate our own conditioning and invites us to actively change our thinking through orienting toward qualities that support peace and the use of affirmations to reset our own thinking. Reading her book has changed me. When I find myself struggling, I think of her and remember her echoing words from *A Course in Miracles*: 'I could see peace instead of this.'"

—Marijke McCandless, *Write Now Mind* and *Juicy Practices for Getting Present* workshop leader, and award-winning author of *More* (written under pen name, Mariah McKenzie)

"Nere Lartitegui's *The Missing Peace* is the kind of book we all need right now. Hopeful and wise, it calls us to be our peaceful selves, with personal stories and helpful takeaways that guide us.

Nere encapsulates the wisdom of more than 80 years, revealing how she moved her own life to one of internal peace. Her message, 'no matter what you have faced in the world, peace is possible.'"

—Marni Freedman, author, writing coach, and co-founder of the San Diego Writers Festival

Part family story, part field guide, *The Missing Peace* shows us, with love and humility, how to access inner peace and return to it when we lose our way. In a time when many of us seek solutions grounded in something other than resentment and fear, this book provides examples and simple tools to guide us toward a sustainable state of inner calm.

—Lindsey Salatka, chronic peace seeker and author of *Fish Heads* and *Duck Skin*

I sincerely recommend *The Missing Peace* by Nere Lartitegui. This book is full of stories and lessons to help us live an intentional peace-centered life using forgiveness, kindness, gratitude, and respect. Nere showed us how to overcome inner, interpersonal, and outer conflicts of our past and present, preserving and enhancing family, friend, and work ties. She encourages us to keep an open heart, set boundaries, use affirmations, and pay attention to opportunities in order to live a happy, fulfilling life. This is a book I will keep on my shelf and re-read often.

—Nancy Mae Johnson, author of *Things My Mama Never Told Me: A Funny and Sometimes Serious Guide For Teen Girls and the People Who Love Them*

The Missing Peace

A GENTLE APPROACH TO FINDING
& MAINTAINING INNER PEACE

Nere Lartitegui, PhD

NLE
PRESS

NLE Press
San Diego, Calif.

Copyright © 2022 Nere Lartitegui
All rights reserved.

No part of this publication may be reproduced, stored in or
introduced into a retrieval system, or transmitted, in any form, or
by any means (electronic, mechanical, photocopying, recording,
or otherwise), without the prior permission of the publisher
except in the case of brief quotations embodied in critical articles
and reviews. Requests for permission should be directed to
readthemissingpeace@gmail.com.

All quotes from *A Course in Miracles* are from the copyright
©1992, 1999, 2007 by the Foundation for Inner Peace,
448 Ignacio Blvd., 306, Novato, CA 94949,
acim.org and info@acim.org, used with permission.

Book Cover and Interior Design by Monkey C Media
Edited by Lyndsey Salatka
Author photo by Captured Forever
All other photos from the Nere Lartitegui collection

First Edition
Printed in the United States of America

ISBN: 979-8-9852956-0-3

Library of Congress Control Number: 2022903077

To everyone who longs
to live a happy, fulfilled,
and peaceful life.

Dear Reader

My intention with *The Missing Peace* is to inspire you to live an authentic life that features peace as its most treasured and indispensable ingredient.

By sharing my life stories and the lessons I learned from surviving tumultuous political upheaval, a heartbreaking divorce, a complete career change, and raising five children, I will walk you through a process of letting go of bitterness, resentment, and victimhood, to allow peace to be the guiding force.

With the use of simple yet effective tools, I hope to inspire you to move from a place of struggle to a place of inner harmony, love, and gratitude. My greatest wish is to open up your eyes to a new way of experiencing life—one full of joy, peace, and fulfillment.

My life has spanned not only more than eight decades but also three distinct cultures and two radically different careers. Yet the course of my life is one that might feel familiar to anyone. On my journey and in this book, I have sought to answer these questions:

What happens when we pursue the things we were told would lead us to fulfillment only to discover that the place we have arrived is unfulfilling? How do we move from that place of dissatisfaction to inner peace? When we face an unwanted situation in life, are we able to recognize the conditioning that may have led us there? Can we dive into that conditioning and rewrite the script?

I was born a child of war in 1936 Basque Country. In 1939, my country was taken over by a dictatorship and my father found himself a target of the new regime. His business was taken away and he was jailed as an enemy of the state. He fled to Venezuela to be able to support us, his family. In 1945, after a difficult five-year separation, our family was reunited and we began a new life together in Venezuela.

For me, an eight-year-old, moving to Venezuela from the Basque Country, the experience was like traveling to the moon—so different was everyday life, not only in geography, but in the nuances of the language, food, and the way people related to each other. In the Basque Country, for instance, the food was mild, spiced primarily with onion and garlic, but the people spoke brusquely. In Venezuela, on the other hand, the people spoke gently, but the food exploded in unknown flavors and spices. It was a lot for a young girl to take in.

As a teenager, with my parents still reeling from the effects of being uprooted, I was strongly encouraged to continue my education in a field that would bring financial security. I didn't pause to consider if this path lit my heart inside; the promise of financial stability was my only consideration. Therefore, I dutifully attended Universidad Central de Venezuela in Caracas, pursued a career in economics, worked in the field, then earned two master's degrees, and eventually became a successful professor of economics. Along the way, I fell in love, got married, and gave birth to five children, fulfilling my maternal dream from childhood.

In 1978, at age forty-one, however, I found myself at a crossroads—my marriage was ending and I realized that my career in economics had not brought me a sense of fulfillment. Everything I thought defined me was no longer working. No one in my family had been through a divorce before, and I had no idea how to create a new life for myself and my five children. I moved temporarily to the United States with my children to pursue a PhD in human behavior and leadership. To get there, I crossed not only physical continents, but the continent of my own broken heart. Amidst the chaos and angst, I was fueled by anger. I blamed my husband for the deep unrest within myself.

Once in the USA, again in a foreign environment, I reached out for help, seeking to reinvent myself. I had begun to recognize that my anger, sadness, and sense of righteousness did not bring me the inner peace and happiness I so deeply desired.

I began to realize I needed to unlearn my deep-seated conditioning. I had worked hard to be a good Catholic woman, wife, mother, and professor of economics, but if I discarded all of these definitions of myself, who was I? I became deeply curious about human nature, how we become the way we are, and what actually brings us happiness and fulfillment.

Alongside laying the groundwork for a new degree while raising my children, I also investigated the nature of unrest inside myself. As I unraveled the sources of my own unhappiness, I began to understand the nature of inner conflict.

Originally embittered by my husband's betrayal, I began to learn about the power of forgiveness, and then the tables started to turn. I began to look inward for happiness and calm, changing my mindset, opening myself up to forgive while actively pursuing opportunities to be happy, rather than unknowingly looking for reasons to stay unhappy.

As I made this pivotal shift, I discovered that my relationships became easier and smoother, and that I felt more connected to my authentic self. With a fulfilling new career path, a changing relationship with my kids and ex-husband, and my active intention to seek contentment, I discovered that peace was possible—and it was an inside job.

While I became 100 percent accountable for my own happiness, the peace inside me slowly grew, as did the qualities fundamental to continue living in peace even when the going gets tough—qualities such as kindness, gratitude, living in the moment, enthusiasm for life, and persistence.

As I grew internally more peaceful, I found myself naturally ready to focus externally on spreading peace, working as a psychotherapist for individuals and groups in the USA and Venezuela for more than ten years. Later I became a conflict resolution mediator and actively worked to create a Department of Peace in our federal government.

This book is the fruit of my journey.

Contents

Introduction

"Let there be peace on earth and let it begin with me."
—JILL JACKSON-MILLER AND SY MILLER

When I began my journey of self-discovery more than forty years ago, I wouldn't have imagined that now, in retrospect, I would assess my discoveries as a sacred path toward sustainable inner peace. The last half of my life so far has been dedicated first to finding that inner peace and then to enhancing it and extending it to my fellow humans through my daily interactions—making it my line of work and sharing it with my family and the people around me. Inner peace is my top priority and most valued goal.

It is my heart's desire to inspire my fellow humans to live an authentic life that includes peace as their most treasured and indispensable ingredient—an umbrella, firmly planted, covering and protecting all. Without the umbrella of peace, many (such as myself in my younger years) might look "successful" according to the world's view, but find ourselves unfulfilled, like something is missing—the inner contentment that allows us to relax and enjoy the fruits of our labor.

1

The journey of life has its ups and downs; all human endeavours do. Instead of being caught in the drama, though, we can become observers; we can learn to center ourselves and navigate life's challenges lightly.

Life can be an amazing school where people and circumstances show up as our teachers just when we need them. Being calm and receptive instead of reactive and defensive helps us discover exactly what we need to learn in each moment.

Even as we look outward and see violence and injustice in the world, when we seek to alleviate it we must remember to first turn our attention inward to embrace the peace within ourselves, so that when we act we are coming from a peaceful place.

So, what does peace look like?

It looks like a normal day, unique to each person except that it is seen through the perspective of peace instead of conflict, which allows us to discover the underlying harmony.

To me it looks like a Sunday morning. I get up early and sip my coffee while reading my intentions and affirmations—a practice I enjoy for its power to center me and help me live that day clearly and to its fullest.

Later, I go for a walk at the nearby park on the shore of the bay, a favorite Sunday activity. I walk slowly and enjoy the view, watching people spending their day off with family and friends. Children, adults, and elders of different ethnicities and body types play, sunbathe, rest, or enjoy lively conversations.

I see life in the park as a micro world, everyone engaging in a favorite activity in harmony. It took me years to realize that what I noticed when I went for a walk was in part a reflection of my own inner peace, rather than a pure observation. Once I had found peace within myself, I saw much more of it reflected around me by people who enjoyed different things from me and added variety to the whole. Even more important, once I upheld reaching for peace as my highest priority and experienced that peace in myself, I naturally extended it to those around me and became instrumental in spreading peace.

Don't worry, dear reader, if you are not already there. Don't worry if you look out and see pain and suffering on your Sunday walk or if you feel upset by people with differing views and lifestyles. The world is evolving, and in many ways it feels unstable. There is judgment and anger all around us; this hampers our sense of security. Social media magnifies these resentments; we can feel them reverberating everywhere. People are struggling; this is real and true. Sometimes your safety must be your utmost concern.

When I began my journey, finding peace looked like an impossible dream as I experienced so much rage, confusion, and self-doubt after my divorce. I had followed the prescribed path to happiness: get a good education, get a good job, get married, have kids. But I wasn't happy. I wasn't at peace. I had to take an inner journey to find peace.

There is much violence, unrest, and injustice in the world today. Sometimes even within our families we are polarized and struggling to find common ground. Maybe you and your family are subjected to that violence and injustice like I was as a child of war. It is understandable if you don't observe a peaceful world on your Sunday walk.

Addressing justice is a necessary first step in working toward social sustainable peace. As a society we *must* address the unrest of the world. But we must not forget that as individuals seeking peace and happiness, we must also address the violence and unrest within ourselves. And, we must recognize that the more peaceful we are inside, the more peace we put out into the world when we seek to address the unrest we find there.

It is important to note that alongside the outer activities we do to correct injustice, there are also things we can do to alter that reality. Together, we can envision a peaceful world, a vision of a world where justice reigns, reparations are made, conflicts are resolved without violence, and the citizens of the world live in harmony. It will take some time—maybe generations—for our vision to come true. In the meantime, we must pursue our most fulfilled and peaceful life and continue to work on ourselves, rooting out the places inside that resist the possibility of peace.

What I came to discover on my long journey is that finding peace can and does overcome suffering. When looking through an eyeglass of peace, I am able to see the situation in front of me clearly without judgment that it is good or bad, but plainly neutral. This openness is important, especially in the beginning of our journey to live peacefully: to accept life and its circumstances as they are without labeling them.

I know this sounds impossible with so much injustice and disharmony in the world now, but the way to peace is accepting what *is* first, and then considering nonviolent solutions as our response. We have plenty of examples of extraordinary people who made this choice: Mahatma Gandhi, Nelson Mandela, Martin Luther King Jr. Legions of ordinary people, like myself, have made this shift too. And it is also available for you.

As a person in my eighties, being an instrument of peace has given me a worthwhile, fulfilling purpose and made me a joyful person. I know that peace is the gem, the most valuable asset I have, and sharing it while interacting with my fellow humans is the most rewarding aspect of my life. I want to share this peace until my last breath.

Because my journey has been that of many women—navigating motherhood and career through heartbreak and difficult external circumstances—I want to share my insights to provide clear and simple steps to make your own path easier. I will offer specific examples of what this looks like during times of outer conflict or inner turmoil.

When we first turn our attention inward in search of the peace already inside ourselves, and then turn outward, we come from a spirit of nonviolence and acceptance of others, embracing, respecting, and appreciating our differences. When we see the beauty of each human experience as being different and valuable, we can discover various and exciting ways to complement each other.

No matter where you are in your life, no matter how much you are struggling, the reality is that you can create a happy, fulfilling, peaceful life, the life you were meant to live.

Join me on this journey to create a calm inner world where you can be, express, and enjoy who you are. This allows us to live in harmony with those with whom we share this precious planet. Just like a Sunday at the park, where everyone is doing their favorite thing and allowing others to enjoy their favorite thing as well.

I am convinced that humanity as a whole is evolving, and it thrills me to consciously be a part of that transformation. By becoming peaceful people, we will naturally contribute to the evolution of humanity.

Part 1

Making a Commitment to Live in Peace

Making a commitment to live in peace is the most valuable goal we can set for ourselves in our relationships, at work, home, and play. When we resolve to include the ingredient of peace, we will set ourselves up to live a more joyful life.

There is a generally accepted correlation between "success" and being famous and rich, often associated with celebrities. That concept of success is misleading; it doesn't include personal fulfillment and contentment with one's accomplishments. Many so-called "successful people" live in inner turmoil and unrest; some even live in deep depression in their lavish lives. I know this because, as you will see, I was one of them.

Chapter 1

The Powerful Practice of Setting Intentions

No matter who we are—rich, poor, famous, or unknown—we are faced with many difficult situations in life. In endeavoring to commit to change—to live a happier, more peaceful life—it is not always clear how to begin. I discovered there is one simple step to start: setting intentions. On my journey, I found that creating an intention, an aspirational goal, is essential in dealing with challenging situations and circumstances and brings me back to peace. Setting an intention narrows my focus so that any decision I make in the face of a challenge is filtered through the new goal. Setting intentions has become the foundation of my journey, something I turn to regularly to jump-start me when I face a new challenge.

Creating an Intention

Late in 2013 I experienced a couple of mini-strokes. My blood pressure spiked, and I felt extremely disoriented but was fortunately without pain.

The consequences of the strokes, however, were quite devastating. My vocal cords were affected. I could not pronounce certain letters and lost my capacity to carry a tune. I could no longer sing in the Threshold Choir with my beloved friends. I also wobbled when I walked and could no longer enjoy strolling by the bay or attending exercise classes. Even driving and running my errands could no longer happen. I began rehabilitation with trainers assisting me at home. I felt helpless. As a strong independent woman, it was difficult for me to be completely reliant on others for all my needs.

In my quiet confinement at home, I found I had a lot of time on my hands. I asked myself, "What can I do beyond my spiritual practices and rehabilitation exercises?" I had some physical issues, but my mind was sharp and clear. I wanted to stay involved and engaged, but I didn't know how. I read some of Ram Dass' teachings, and his words inspired me to open up to receive what was next for me. I decided to create an intention for the upcoming year of 2014. This is what came to me:

"I, Nere, now open myself to your sweet inspiration to use my time to love, serve, and remember in the capacity that will be more appropriate and convenient for me. Activities, people, and circumstances are coming to me at the right time, and I can see them. Thank you, Beloved. I surrender to your loving guidance."

Fervently I read that intention daily and felt in my heart it would become true without having a clue how it would materialize.

In January, not even two months after the strokes, my daughters, Nere and Verónica, asked me to participate in a study group they were creating using the self-teaching book on spiritual psychotherapy, *A Course in Miracles*. I consider myself a lifetime student of *A Course;* I had begun studying it thirty years before, in the early eighties. I felt honored by the surprising invitation from my daughters. From the spiritual wisdom we shared to the questions and perspective each person contributed, this group was a wonderful chapter of my life, and after five years, we satisfactorily concluded it.

My clear intention opened me up to receive new opportunities, allowing me to participate in a life-changing experience with some of my loved ones.

The Origin of the Disturbance

Sometimes, more work must be done to get to the root of the problems we face. We may recognize that we are not at peace because we feel agitated or emotionally upset about something, without knowing exactly why. It helps to set an intention to find what I think of as "the origin of the disturbance." This may require a period of quiet reflection. Such was the case with me as 2014 advanced.

As I had recently set my intention to surrender to loving guidance after the mini strokes, I paid close attention to what came up. Thus, when my dear friend Mnimaka told me about an eight-week webinar on how to improve the quality of our lives, I signed up, eager to participate, learn, and grow. A couple of weeks into the class I realized I wanted to heal a disturbing memory: When my children casually mentioned their deceased dad in our conversations, hurtful memories of the ugly end of our marriage would assault me and spoil the moment. It felt like a punch in my gut that took my breath away. The divorce had happened thirty-five years earlier, yet those memories still haunted me.

Week after week I kept reflecting, writing, and sharing my discoveries. By the end of the webinar I had a new perspective of my marriage and its end. I realized my marriage had a purpose defined by the five children we both loved and cared for. After that, our reason to be together was completed. We completed our marriage contract—not for life, as I had thought, but for the time needed. Then, we were free to go our separate ways. Since our divorce, I have greatly benefited from being on my own. Starting in 1978, I embarked on giving birth to the real Nere, the authentic me, away from the roles I played as a wife and economist; every day the new Nere was released from old habits, conditioning, and self-imposed limitations.

Healing my fixation on the last year of my marriage also allowed me to remember the previous nineteen years I spent with Enrique. Most of the memories were pleasant, uplifting, and made me smile. Now my marriage memories allow me to see our time together as a significant and successful adventure that provided me with Nere, Enrique, Pascual, Verónica, and

Ignacio, my beloved five children and personal teachers in this lifetime.

We can create an intention to change the course of any specific struggle we are experiencing internally or externally. We can also set an intention to discover the origin of the disturbance, as I did in the example above. Intentions are powerful tools that help us focus our energy toward a desired outcome. I use them constantly. At the present moment, I have written intentions that I read daily to improve my relationships with my kids and with my finances, to complete writing my book to my satisfaction, and to live joyfully in my eighties.

I have found the beauty of setting intentions to be contagious. People love to see how someone is actively changing their life for the better through the simple use of intentions, and when they catch on, it is a joy to see their power at work in those around us.

Early in 2020, my granddaughter Viviana graduated from Emerson College with a degree in journalism. Soon she moved to Los Angeles to search for a job. When the pandemic hit and put her life on hold, she moved back to her parents' home in San Diego. She was anxious about her future, especially about finding a decent job in the middle of the pandemic. With those unsettling thoughts attacking her constantly, it was hard for her to relax and enjoy the company of her beloved younger sister Valeria or her loving parents who cherished her.

In one of our conversations, I suggested I could assist her in creating an intention to find a job from a place of calm and assurance. By the middle of May it was completed. In her written intention she declared her perfect job existed, and that she would discover and land it. She envisioned herself excited about directing all she learned to serve others to the best of her ability. She asked in return to be paid enough to easily cover all her living expenses. After some more specifics, we finished by thanking the Universe in advance for her perfect job as if it was already accomplished. Viviana was able to read her intention to find her job every day until her job manifested.

As time passed, her demeanor changed from serious and disengaged to relaxed, smiling, and present. The special bond between the two sisters increased; I often saw them giggling and laughing.

On September 1, Viviana began working in Los Angeles with four preschool children to keep them engaged with their Zoom classes and to teach them Spanish. She made enough money to support herself and rent an apartment with three good friends from college. This is not her dream work, but it's a beginning, and she is happy to be living independently with her close friends in her chosen city. She has returned to peace and contentment.

All of us have the ability to reach peace, even when it feels impossible. It is important to first look at the origin of the disturbance, then direct your inner power to change it. In creating your intention, use only affirmative statements, clearly focusing on what you want, not on what you lack. Use present tense, as it is happening now, not in the future, and conclude by thanking the Universe or Higher Power for manifesting your intention.

Sharing Your Intentions

To make your intention even more powerful, share it with others.

There is a simple and powerful ritual called the Stone Ceremony that serves as a way to share your intentions with a group. I learned it from Unity Fellowship Church, a non-denominational spiritual center in San Diego where they perform the Stone Ceremony every December. Some years ago we incorporated this ritual into our family, and it has added greater cohesiveness and intimacy among us. You can use it in groups with some affinity, like a book club, a hiking club, or a special project group.

I met with my family for this ritual on my eighty-third birthday. The twelve of us sat in an informal circle outside our vacation accommodation in Valle de Guadalupe. Each one of us had prepared in advance one word that summarized what we wanted to accomplish in 2020. I invited everyone to share and explain their chosen word for 2020, and also to tell us how their 2019 words had worked for them.

The discussion was honest, with everyone opening up about their inner world to the rest of the group. The contributions from the four grandkids, ages nine to twenty-two, were especially uplifting; they gave us the opportunity to listen and cheer them on as they shared the deepest desires of their youthful hearts. After each person spoke, the rest of us affirmed the word for that person for the new year as though it had already happened. Explore, transformation, action, and harmony were some of the chosen words, among others.

My daughter-in-law, Marianna, chose harmony. The year before, she had begun a full-time job that created some disruption in the routine of her family as she was no longer a full-time mother and housewife. I chose tolerance. My loved ones have pointed out to me that sometimes I am intolerant and force my point of view on others, especially if I am passionate about an issue. I want to respect everyone in thoughts and words, so tolerance was my focus for my personal growth that year. I want to live, but also I want to let everyone live in the way that makes the most sense for them.

The Stone Ceremony

Below is a simple ritual to perform with a group of people to enhance your practice of setting intentions. The ritual seems quite simple and playful, but you might be surprised by its powerful effect.

- Pull together a group of friends with a common bond.
- Gather a collection of small stones and some paint.
- Invite each person to come up with a single word that synthesizes what he or she wants to accomplish in the new year.
- Decorate each stone with one word plus some colorful artwork as a reminder throughout the year.
- Share with each other and receive reinforcement from the group.

I think you'll find that sharing single word intentions and creating colorful playful reminders creates room to initiate thoughtful conversations throughout the year between members of the group about how each is manifesting their chosen word. Having the loving energy of a group is an extra boost to begin a new, adventurous year. We are held accountable by others to remember our own highest goal. As the Three Musketeers say, *All for one and one for all.*

Even though the origin of our ceremony was inspired by "The White Stone Ceremony" performed at the Unity Center, when my family performed the ceremony, we changed and adapted it to the wants and needs of our group. You also can customize the Stone Ceremony to your specific group. Surely, it will add depth to your normal encounters knowing what each person wants most for themselves.

Always remember, it doesn't need to be hard. A little willingness takes you a long way. Your willingness to not compromise your inner peace and keeping it as your number one priority will attract situations to deepen and increase your contentment and joy.

Invitation

1. I invite you to own your personal power to create your future and refuse to see yourself as a victim of people or circumstances. We all have a choice in how we respond to any situation. We can do nothing and feel depressed and victimized, or, with courage, we can open ourselves up, accept our power, and choose our highest good. By choosing our best, we can return to contentment and peace of mind, our most valuable asset.

2. When you are ready, consider making this simple intention:

   "From today on, I (insert your first name) declare that living in peace with myself is my number one priority."

Part 2

Qualities Conducive to Maintaining Peace

S ome human qualities are fundamental in order to experience peace as our steady state of being. These include forgiveness, kindness, gratitude, respect, living in the moment, persistence, and enthusiasm. Embracing these qualities will sometimes require making a 180-degree turn. Other times, we already have a natural tendency to live and express them, or we may be somewhere in between. In any case, it is valuable to practice these qualities and be aware of their importance in living a peaceful life. It does not matter how far along we are in applying them; what matters is our willingness to embrace these qualities as a personal choice and not as another mandatory rule to follow.

Be gentle with yourself. Remember, once again, we are all students in the school of life, and making mistakes is part of our learning process. We only need to have compassion for ourselves and make corrections as we go along.

It is important to accept life as a journey and keep practicing our chosen values as best we can. As I write this, I am in my eighties and have been on a peaceful path for half of my life. However, I still make mistakes that can disturb me and those around me. The saving grace is that I accept that I can—and likely will—make mistakes sometimes. My path forward is to acknowledge the mistakes as soon as I see them, correct them, and when needed, apologize.

Recently, I went to pick up a rental car I had reserved. The employee told me they didn't have the car at that moment, and I got upset. I said, "I cannot believe a prestigious firm like this would allow this to happen. I reserved the car yesterday. If there is an issue, the least I expect is to be called and told, to spare us from coming."

My daughter Verónica, who drove me there, looked at me and told me to calm down. I listened to her and stopped, remembering I can be intense when disappointed. I realized that he was just an employee; he was not responsible for his company's mistakes, he was only the messenger of the bad news. I apologized profusely, and then, back on good terms, we made another deal that worked well. The interaction lasted a matter of minutes when I shifted my approach and took responsibility for the impact of my reaction on the employee and returned to a cordial exchange.

Making mistakes keeps us humble about our human frailties. Apologizing for our mistakes when another person is involved is the just way to conclude an error; it helps both parties return to calm and harmony.

Let's take a quick peek at the qualities mentioned above before we dive in deeper.

Forgiveness is at the base of all qualities. We cannot free ourselves from the past while remaining attached to our anger, resentment, hurtful feelings, and the desire to retaliate.

Kindness helps us to move away from our ego, putting our attention on the well-being of others and enjoying the inner satisfaction it brings.

Gratitude keeps us in the present moment, allowing us to change our focus from what we lack to what we have.

Respect rests on the belief that all humans deserve to be honored for no other reason than being born, equalizing the worth of all human beings.

Living in the moment means being focused on what is happening right now, rather than on a story in our head from yesterday or tomorrow.

Persistence is the inner strength that propels us to continue our pursuit of what is important to us even if it takes longer or is more complex than we thought.

Enthusiasm is the vibrancy, the passion we feel inside and exude when we are pursuing what is important to us.

These qualities are interrelated, and taking a step forward in one can enhance another, like how being present in the moment keeps us from worrying about tomorrow's job interview, which in turn can increase simple gratitude for witnessing an amazing sunset. Each quality can offer an alternate response to a situation and enhance the quality of our peaceful living.

Let's dive deeper.

Chapter 2
Forgiveness

I address forgiveness first because it is the most important quality to cultivate and the foundation for all the rest. Bottom line—holding onto grudges and feeling like others are our enemies or the causes of our strife results in unrest and unhappiness. Forgiveness frees us from past hurts. Nevertheless, it can be challenging. It was for me.

My own journey to forgiveness began after my traumatic divorce from my husband of fifteen years and the father of my five children. Forgiveness did not happen overnight; it took time. Initially, I had strong emotions, especially righteousness, anger, and fear. I needed time to grieve what I had lost. After a while, I adopted a curious attitude about moving past my feelings of helpless victimhood, and became open to new ways of thinking. I had to look at my own conditioning that was keeping me stuck in a position of victimhood. This shift included seeking professional help to get past my angry feelings. Since day one, my intuition led me to develop my own set of ground rules for dealing with the situation, which included practicing non-retaliation, not bad-mouthing my ex to the kids, and eventually working in a spirit of collaboration with him for our kids' well-being. But I also practiced important and alternative healing resources, especially breathwork, and studied *A Course in Miracles*, which I will touch on later.

Although my story is unique to me, many elements are universal. It is common to live under certain assumptions and with certain beliefs that are unexpectedly uprooted and challenged at their core.

Enrique and I met as volunteers in a Catholic association for college students in Caracas, working in the *barrios* with underprivileged people. Our convictions were strong and similar, and our marriage was based on the belief it would last "until death do us part." Divorce did not cross my mind; I never contemplated it as a possibility for us.

A year before the divorce, we went through some difficulties in our marriage. Our communication had faltered, so we initiated marriage counseling and formally recommitted to staying together, no matter what, and making the necessary changes. I faithfully followed the counsel, giving the best of myself to save our marriage. Then a good friend of ours opened my eyes to what was happening behind my back. Enrique had been having an affair with a woman, another friend of ours, for more than two years. Shocked, I realized he had been consistently lying to me.

After confirming his betrayal and finding myself unable to trust him anymore, I decided to get divorced.

Before my decision, we had been planning to move to San Diego as a family. I was to pursue a PhD in human behavior and leadership, my recently found and cherished field of interest, while Enrique would use his sabbatical to further his education. After deciding to divorce, we moved forward with the plan to go to San Diego, but separately. I would live with our children and Enrique would live on his own.

I reasoned that a new start in an unfamiliar place might be a good way for me to distract myself from my anguish and focus on a new chapter. I wanted to move forward with integrity and follow my convictions. Moving to the USA worked well because it created a physical distance from some women in Venezuela who were well-meaning in their support but emphatically counseled me to retaliate against Enrique. They wanted me to take the kids away from him and hurt him financially—to seek revenge. But their opinions never resonated with me. Instinctively, I knew that taking revenge against my husband was not my path. I didn't know it at the time, but this inner desire *not* to seek revenge was my first step of my future intention to live in peace.

I could have stayed in my familiar surroundings fueling my hurt self, but I felt called to change my environment for a new and unknown and also to follow my heart's desire with my education. So, at forty-one, I moved with my five children to San Diego, California, in search of a new beginning. I was determined to mend my broken heart while creating a new and satisfying career and desperately searching for inner peace. I didn't know how, but instinctively I knew that taking revenge against my husband was not my path. In the seven transformational years to follow in San Diego, I diligently searched for and ultimately found my real self and the inner peace that I cultivated as my most valuable asset.

The beginning was not easy. I went from sadness to rage to confusion to hopelessness and back again, all while raising my five kids in a new culture and attending graduate school for my PhD in psychology.

I experienced disparate moods and emotions throughout each day. With my peers at school and socially with my new friends I felt confident; I was always looking for a chance to tell the story of the end of my marriage and how I was discarded like an old pair of shoes. Venting made me feel powerful—at least temporarily.

In the mornings, while I was studying at home and my kids were at school, I would break down, a weeping mess. My inner voice nagged: *I can't make it alone. And with five children? Impossible. I don't have what it takes to create a sustainable, happy life for my kids and me.* Feeling victimized, I would cry and sob, mourning the end of my marriage, full of doubts and despair for a future on my own—far from the peace I desired. In the early afternoon, however, I would take a shower to reduce the redness and swelling of my face and put on a smile before my kids came home.

At dinnertime, I focused on paying attention to my kids, listening to their stories about school life. I knew from my experience adapting to Venezuela as a child that they just needed to be heard so they could continue in their adaptation to America. I didn't express to them my aggressive feelings toward their father or my doubts about our future. I wanted them to live fully in their own moment without the burden of my sorrow.

That was the first phase after divorce. It was a chaotic and difficult time, day after day, like riding a rollercoaster that took me from anger and rage, to doubt, to deep sadness and despair. I came to see this was a necessary stage in my grief. I needed to be able to feel my anger and vent it to move past what I thought my life was about.

As I transitioned into fully accepting my new life as a single mother, my need to vent and blame naturally began to diminish, helped along by the growing intention—the one that first showed up as a tiny whisper encouraging me to move—to seek peace instead of conflict. I began to see that feeling like a victim was not serving my higher goal.

With a curious attitude, I began searching for ways to decondition myself from feeling like a helpless victim. As a victim, I would strike out verbally blaming my ex-husband, which momentarily felt good, but ultimately didn't bring me to a place of wholeness and peace inside myself. Victimhood left me feeling anxious and powerless instead of what I wanted, which was to feel strong and capable of taking control of my own life.

I started therapy to express and release my distress and rage, instead of venting in social circles. It worked well in stopping the victim story inside my head and opening me up to assume responsibility for my own happiness. I also honored myself for the good choices I was making. I realized that while I was subject to my own conditioning and victim identity, I also had inner wisdom gently guiding me.

We all have inner wisdom, but sometimes it is drowned out by the screaming, blaming ego. When we begin on the path of forgiveness and healing, it is important to discern what is our own intuition—our inner knowing—and separate this from our conditioned beliefs. It can be tricky to separate the two, but know this: *inner wisdom is kind, it does not blame and does not seek revenge.*

On my path, I adopted three practical tools that came from tuning into my own intuition (inner wisdom) and stemmed from my commitment to the well-being of my five children. These were crucial to initiate the long process of forgiveness. I share them here because they are universally helpful. But I encourage you to look inside and honor your own inner wisdom too. What sage, kind words of advice does your heart speak?

Three Tools: Non-retaliation, No Bad-mouthing, Collaboration

The three practical tools that helped me to successfully initiate and progress in my path were these: non-retaliation, no bad-mouthing, and becoming a parent team with my ex.

1. Non-retaliation

Even in the midst of my rage against my ex-husband and despite the insistence of some women back in Venezuela, I never felt drawn to follow the path of retaliation. Recognizing this within myself provided a first step in my healing.

Embarking on a war and recruiting five innocent children to fight against their father was not my path.

I kept hearing a voice: *Nere, you can be a good, bad, or so-so mother, but you cannot be a father. Your kids deserve to have a father. Do whatever you need to allow them this fundamental relationship. Never be an obstacle.*

A crucial part of my upbringing was having a caring, protective father whom I adored. His guidance was a main pillar in the strong values of my character. I wanted my kids to have this opportunity with their father too, without my interference.

I accepted this voice as my guide while embarking on the long process of searching for my authentic self.

2. No bad-mouthing

Closely related to non-retaliation, I promised myself to never bad-mouth their dad to my kids, no matter how angry I felt. I kept reminding myself that my kids were also his, and that bad-mouthing him was stepping between each of them and their father, interfering with the relationship each of them deserved.

It was difficult to stay on course, day after day, while anger and aggressive feelings bubbled up inside me, and I often felt the urgent need to let them spill out. But I was convinced that not denigrating him was essential to allowing my kids to continue relating to their dad in a direct, healthy way. That decision was the most difficult one to follow, a lot harder than the courses for the PhD I was studying. I am grateful for this choice as it brought incredible benefits to my family.

3. Collaboration

The third choice came about from the fact that my five children needed lots of support as they began their lives in a new country, learning a new language, adapting to school, and making new friends. Enrique and I developed a new way of relating—as single parents. The fact that our children's well-being was a priority for both of us was our single reason to stay connected. We frequently met to talk about our kids and decide what each one needed in terms of support from us. This required me to put aside my personal baggage and bring out my best to team up with Enrique for our kids' benefit. Reflecting on that time now amazes me—I was able to do that in the midst of my inner turmoil. My ex and I became a team to support our kids in the best way we knew how.

These three tools were practical ways for me to stop fighting the situation and disarm myself. Finding peace requires stopping the war, and I was doing that to benefit my kids. In this, I was peeling that first layer of forgiveness that allowed me to feel more at ease and quieter inside, and begin the process of accessing my own inner peace. I was the first beneficiary of my own disarming.

Now, more than fifteen years after my ex's death, my kids have great memories of him and hold him up as the greatest dad. They allowed me to discover a failed husband could be a great father.

In addition to my own practical tools, I also sought the wisdom of others. On my journey, I found a powerful breathing technique that, along with *A Course in Miracles,* ended up being fundamental in my healing and reprogramming. I was pleased to discover that *A Course* reinforced what I had already begun to notice by following my own intuition and developing my three tools to stop the warring with my ex-husband. *A Course* calls this a "little willingness" to open up to Spirit. We all have such inner wisdom. We just need to receive it and use it with confidence.

A Course and breathwork therapy planted me solidly on the path to forgiveness and allowed me to find my inner peace while discovering my true self.

Breathwork Therapy

When I investigated the many healing resources available in San Diego, I discovered a breathwork therapy called rebirthing, which was a powerful tool in the process of healing myself. It is called "rebirthing" because it was initially associated with recreating and reprogramming a traumatic birth experience through breathwork. Eventually, rebirthing came to refer to a more general form of voluntary breathwork therapy that was found to help release old stuck emotions.

During a rebirthing session, either in a group or individually, a guide coaches the participants to breathe in a continual circular breathing pattern. It is a little like a guided meditation session, but it focuses solely on using voluntary breath to interrupt the body's normal conditioning by bringing the body into an altered state. This is very effective in causing emotions to rise and be released. I consistently practiced rebirthing for many years, releasing old hurts through the breath, and observing the healing effect of rebirthing on others when I became a coach myself, a "rebirther."

At the end of each rebirthing session, we fill the inner vacuum created with affirmative truths, such as "I, Nere, see and embrace my innocence," or "I, Nere, deserve to be loved." Reading and writing these affirmations daily prompted me to pursue happiness as my birthright.

There are many different modalities of using the power of the breath to release past hurts available. If you choose one of them, make sure to take it under the care of a reliable professional.

A Course in Miracles

My first rebirthing practitioner introduced me to *A Course in Miracles,* a powerful spiritual and psychological book published in 1977 that was instrumental in turning my life around and still clarifies and directs me in my evolution today.

The book was hard to understand at first. With patience and persistence, plus the ongoing support of my teachers at the World Healing Center, I learned powerful lessons in small doses. I became a humble life student of *A Course,* learning and healing myself, one day at a time.

I learned that forgiveness was the key element to becoming the calm and happy person I wanted to be, though at the time it looked like an out-of-reach goal. *A Course* asserts that offering forgiveness to others and to ourselves is the only way to attain peace. In lesson 121, the book states, "Forgiveness is the key to happiness," and "Here is the answer to your search for peace."

The teachings of *A Course* profoundly resounded in me. Some of them were the opposite of the religious teachings I had held onto for so long. Instead of seeing life as a valley of tears where we suffer and work hard to access a happy afterlife, *A Course* proclaims happiness is our divine inheritance right now.

I had been taught that everyone is a sinner from conception, in need of repenting for our lifelong sins. *A Course* affirms once and again the innocence of all human beings, and says sins are the invention of the ego to make us feel guilty and undeserving. We humans commit errors—mistakes, but not sins—and errors call for correction, not for punishment.

This gave me clarity. Instead of seeing Enrique as an evil person who purposely hurt me, I could now see him as a person who made a mistake, maybe a big one to me, but nevertheless, a mistake. This laid a pathway for empathy toward him and kindness toward myself because I, too, make mistakes. It also opened the door to forgiveness.

Forgiveness required me to not only stop judging him and holding grudges against him, but also to see him as innocent. This was easier said than done. Innocent? That seemed an impossible conclusion, but with my newfound insight, I persisted.

I began to see that it was my own obsessive blaming thoughts that kept me suffering, not Enrique's behavior. The process of my forgiveness took years. I had to disentangle my real self from the ego that held onto the grudges that kept me bound to the past. This was the beginning of my journey in replacing old beliefs, learning to listen to myself, and taking responsibility for my own happiness.

I faced a long and complex forgiveness process that required peeling my conditioning one layer at a time. It was at the base of healing myself so I could discover and live the peaceful life I was born to live without further delays.

You, dear reader, must discern for yourself what resonates within you. The goal is to find a path that encourages you to stop blaming and playing the victim and instead empower yourself to take responsibility in creating your own happiness. If you see yourself in need and wanting to forgive, you will find a way to achieve it.

Instead of using our energy to blame, condemn, and feed our anger, which keeps us victimized, we need to focus on our expansion, and in doing so, we will liberate ourselves. We all can do this. Through forgiveness we can release the person and use that energy to create our own reality. Forgiving others is actually self-serving as it unburdens and frees us, allowing us to move on and reach our goals. Instead of fixating on what happened in the past, we can focus on the present, where we will create a life that will make us happy and at peace.

I ask you: Is there any person you need to forgive? Who would be the most difficult person for you to not feel anger toward? Is it a parent or family member, a boss or co-worker, an ex-partner or spouse?

This is who you should focus on forgiving. Follow your intuition to find your way and apply the tools accordingly. Remember it is about disarming yourself. By freeing yourself from the burden of hate, you can move forward in peace, and this is the greatest gift you can give yourself.

Invitation

1. In the process of forgiveness, accept the likelihood of strong emotions, especially righteousness and fear.

2. Accept and allow a period of grief as part of the journey.

3. Become curious about moving past victimhood and be open to new ideas.

4. Seek professional help, if needed, to get past feelings of anger or helplessness.

5. Pay attention and follow your intuition. Before making decisions, we can ask ourselves, *Is this action going to bring the sense of calm that I really want? Will this negatively affect others?*

6. Create your own peace-oriented ground rules.

7. Search and try solutions that may be available and resonate with you.

8. Remember it is human to make mistakes. Looking at others as human beings who make mistakes helps us accept our own failings, which is essential to our healing journey.

Chapter 3

Kindness

Kindness helps us keep and enhance peace in our life. Kindness changes our self-centered orientation and refocuses our attention on contributing to the well-being of others. At the same time it gives us inner satisfaction and peace. In other words, it feels good to be kind.

As humans, I believe we are all born decent and good, but there are ways to increase our basic level of kindness. Paying attention and reflecting on what happens to us makes this easier.

I will take you through my own journey to becoming a kinder person, and how my journey increased my appreciation of this human quality.

In my teens, I possessed the dangerous combination of a sharp mind, a confused heart, and a full ego. When facing someone with a differing opinion, I would use all my fighting skills to put that person down, often with a big dose of sarcasm. This made me feel superior and triumphant. Friends and family often cheered me on for my sharp wit and ability to defeat an opponent verbally and decisively. While I noticed the triumphant feeling never lasted, I would quickly dismiss any hint of remorse that arose.

All of that changed when I met Enrique, my future husband. I was twenty when we fell in love. In response to my frequent verbal duels, and while my usual cheering squad applauded my sharp tongue, it surprised me that Enrique remained serious and quiet.

One time, after another one of my verbal smackdowns, we sat quietly alone. Softly he asked, "Nere, how do you think that person felt after talking to you?"

I made excuses for why the other person deserved what I told him and tried to discard Enrique's question. Yet the question stayed with me. It knocked on the door of my real self.

We were madly in love, and Enrique's opinions were important to me. Enrique's innocent question, plus his lack of reinforcement of my outbursts, made me question the way I was interacting with the people around me. In a powerful and peaceful way he made me realize how my words could hurt others.

My ego fought and tried to survive but in truth, I could feel it dying little by little. Then the day came when I faced a person who held a different belief than mine, and I no longer fought. I no longer found value in inflicting pain on others so I could feel a momentary winning boost. Instead I noticed I felt calmer and happier when I didn't go for the win. It was the beginning of experiencing for myself the power of kindness.

I had been acting from the position that demonstrating how smart I was would make me happy. I was wrong.

The unlearning began when I stopped seeing myself on a battlefield, fighting an enemy and needing to win. I began to change my perspective and share my ideas with others, exchanging our thoughts on issues to have a more complete, rounded understanding. I was not competing against them but working with them, and together, finding the best way to move forward.

The beauty of this new path was that it allowed me to see others and myself on the same journey toward happiness and fulfillment and it came with a glowing, pervasive, peaceful feeling that I hadn't had before. A new paradigm opened up: I win when everyone else wins with me. This was a life-changing lesson and became a mantra that guides my interaction with others: Make it a win-win for everybody.

Years later, I read in *A Course in Miracles* a succinct question we can ask ourselves summing up what I had discovered from Enrique's gentle guidance. The question is: *Do you prefer to be right or happy?*

Occasionally I find myself reacting in the old way—needing to be right. But I try to catch myself, remembering how collaborating with others is an expansive experience that benefits everyone, especially myself.

I admit I have a temper. I am glad it doesn't come up very often any more. Now, most of the time, I catch myself before I explode and take a couple of deep breaths to calm myself. Once in a while I lose control and shout something I immediately regret, realizing it was offensive. When this happens, I make a point to apologize for my behavior, acknowledging my human frailty.

A sincere, humble apology, such as in the example at the car rental agency, can quickly restore relationships. Like anything else, practice improves the expression of our apologies. Changing behavior takes time and practice. It requires unlearning old, detrimental behaviors. We need to be kind with ourselves, too, gently forgiving ourselves when we stumble, then stand up and continue.

Twenty years ago I received a postcard from a friend with a saying from the Dalai Lama: "My religion is very simple. My religion is kindness." Those words struck a chord deep inside, and I told myself that was exactly how I wanted to live. From that moment on I knew that kindness would be my religion too—and by that, I mean it is something I want to practice continuously.

Opportunities for kindness are in front of us all the time, even during normal daily tasks like going to work, driving, cleaning, or cooking. When we adjust our perspective to include people around us, whether they are family, coworkers, friends, or total strangers, our interaction with them can be mutually rewarding. And when conflict arises, we can take a long breath and ask ourselves, *Do I want to be right or happy?* Choosing happiness is a win-win.

Kindness is a natural application of the golden rule, the expression of a high regard for others in the way we treat them.

Invitation

1. Pay attention to your own behavior. Is there some way that you instinctively react that might not serve you anymore? Have you considered how your behavior might affect others? Ask yourself whether you would rather be right or happy, and then reflect on the impact of that realization.

2. Consider whether you have approached verbal exchanges as a battlefield where there are winners and losers. When we let go of the ego's need to be right and, instead, steer a conversation to thoughts on the issues, both parties can enrich their perspective and "win." Check in with how this approach makes you feel in the long run.

3. Remember to be kind with yourself and gently forgive yourself when you stumble and make a mistake. Changing behaviors is courageous and takes time and practice.

4. When you notice you have allowed anger or mean words to rule, swiftly apologize and then let it go. A fast and humble apology can easily restore relationships, as the other person can relate to their own human frailties.

Chapter 4
Gratitude

G ratitude is an attitude of appreciation toward life's gifts. It is about valuing what we have. For that to happen we need to see what is in front of us, not only with our physical eyes but also with our hearts. When our mind is preoccupied, we are not fully present in the moment and we miss opportunities to experience gratitude. But gratitude gives our lives depth and enhances our connection with others, which in turn increases our happiness.

When I was growing up in Venezuela, my mom often tried to instill gratitude in my sister and myself. As a teenager I strongly resisted these reminders. *Don't tell me what to do, don't tell me how to feel,* I thought, *There is so much I lack, why would I be grateful?* I blocked myself to gratitude with disdain and impatience, thinking I knew better. Instead of living in a middle-class apartment in downtown Caracas, I wanted us to live in a house in the suburbs like most of my classmates. When we moved to our dream house in the suburbs, I continued comparing myself with my friends, feeling deprived for not having something else I wanted. Because I was preoccupied with fitting in with the Venezuelan culture, I was missing the many gifts life was presenting me.

My lack of gratitude changed for the better when I first moved to the USA.

It was 1965 when my husband Enrique and I moved to Philadelphia for less than two years so we could both pursue master's degrees in economics. We had two children at the time: Nere was two years old and Enrique was four months old.

One day, while I was washing a bunch of apples in the sink, an unexpected wave of appreciation came over me for our abundance. It's not that I had anything more than I had before—I was a twenty-eight-year-old married graduate student with young kids, living off our scholarships. It's just that I suddenly saw what I *did* have. It was a singular and important moment in my life when my heart opened up and allowed me to appreciate my abundance.

The difference was not outside in the material world, but inside of me. As I changed my perception, I changed my attitude. The impact of this simple moment of pure gratitude influenced the rest of my life. It opened me up to value my life instead of taking all I had for granted. At that moment, I felt deeply satisfied. Somehow, the apples were a portal for me to notice, acknowledge, and be grateful for the abundance in my life.

Later that year, in November, my gratitude attitude substantially increased again. Through the University of Pennsylvania we chose a program for foreigners that paired us with a host family, an American couple with young children like us. From helping us find the right pediatrician to picnicking together in fun parks and everything in between, their inclusion made our stay smoother and more fun.

They invited us to celebrate Thanksgiving in their home with a traditional turkey dinner with all the trimmings, preceded by a prayer of thanks for the abundance and blessings received throughout the year. After the prayer, we shared what we were thankful for. I said, "I am thankful to you for providing us with this intimate and potent way to share gratitude with our loved ones."

That was my first Thanksgiving, and I will never forget what a profound impact it had on me, providing another opening to appreciate life gifts. *What a great country this is that stops one day a year to be collectively grateful,* I thought. We were so impressed that my family enthusiastically adopted the annual celebration when we returned to Venezuela. Now, no matter where we live, we celebrate this holiday with gusto, inviting relatives and friends to join us in thankfulness.

Once I opened my heart to the idea of gratitude, not as something I *should* do, but something I was pleased to experience, I began to seek out moments where I could feel that powerful feeling. And what I've learned is this: It's never too late to open our hearts to gratitude, whether we are experiencing a new culture or other circumstances. Gratitude is a simple way to see the same thing with different eyes. I remember now to pause, and pay attention—to allow myself to be flooded with gratitude for what I have. It's not about the quantity. Everywhere there are people with more and less than me. When I focus on what I have, instead of looking at what

I lack, I feel grateful, and I feel at peace. And when I feel at peace, I love what and who I am.

For some time, I kept a gratitude journal. At the end of every day I came up with five things I was grateful for. Every day I tried to incorporate new things, instead of repeating the same things from previous days. I highly recommend this. Practice makes perfect, especially in adopting a new habit like gratitude.

One of my favorite songs, *Gracias a la Vida, Thanks to Life,* is a hymn of gratitude to life, reminding us to be thankful for our eyes, our ears, our feet, our hearts with all the possibilities to use them to enrich our life experiences.

Meister Eckart, the thirteenth-century German mystic, said: "If the only prayer you say is thank you, it will be enough." We can be inspired to be more grateful by listening to specific songs, reading quotes, and surrounding ourselves with examples of gratitude.

Invitation

1. Consider whether you have innate obstacles to feeling gratitude. Has gratitude become something other people think you should experience?

2. Pay attention to any natural moment when a feeling of gratitude washes over you.

3. Begin to seek out moments where you might experience gratitude.

4. A gratitude journal is helpful to create the habit of being thankful. Listening to songs and reading quotes on gratitude can inspire us to expand our gratitude.

Chapter 5

Respect

Respect involves accepting people for who they are—different and unique—with their own opinions and ways of being. Being respectful offers others the space to be themselves. Often, in our deepest relationships, we forget to respect each other. We wish others would think more like us, be more like us, live more like us. We may even struggle so much with the way others feel or think that we conclude we cannot find a space of peace with them. It doesn't help that respect for differing opinions is not nurtured in our current society. Looking around, we seem to nurture grudges, fighting, pointing fingers, and blaming. Many people go to their corners and do not even try to communicate with respect. This raises the question: Are we, as a society, losing respect for respect? Can we ever regain the crucial ability to honor others who are different from ourselves?

The answer is yes. In fact, it is exactly in times like these that we must lean into respect more than ever. We have experienced what our world is like without respect. It hurts; it's painful. Choosing to live with respect for one another can open our hearts, create new opportunities, and foster an ongoing sense of inner peace.

People deserve respect simply because they are human, independent of how they use their time in this world. However, sometimes the word "respect" is reserved to express appreciation for people's accomplishments. What I am referring to is a deeper, primordial acknowledgement.

This attitude of respect goes hand in hand with inner peace. When we respect and appreciate the lives of others, this sentiment naturally reflects back on ourselves. In the safe harbor we cultivate, where each of us can express our uniqueness, we create inner relaxation. By allowing others to be true to themselves and giving ourselves the same gift, we acknowledge that on some level we are all doing the best we can with the cards we were dealt. For example, if a friend is late for dinner, we can respect the person by assuming it was for a good reason. Respect implies assuming the best intentions of people.

While it took me a while to fully accept peace as my primary focus, I learned about the importance of respect many years earlier when my kids were still small children.

Like many, as a girl I dreamed of having my own family with many lively children running around and playing with each other. When the time was ripe, I bore five healthy children. Even though they were my childhood dream, I made my share of mistakes raising them. I found myself often impatient and angry instead of enjoying the time. Sometimes I screamed at them and even pushed them. I couldn't understand why they didn't act the way I expected them to, why they didn't respond to situations the way I wanted them to. Why wouldn't they go to bed when I told them to? Why wouldn't they stop fighting, finish their dinner, and be quiet?

At the time, I believed that in order for our household to be happy, I needed to mold my kids; I needed them to see that my way of doing something was the "right" way, and they just needed to obey. Bedtime was when they should say goodnight and go to bed without protesting, lingering, or making excuses to stay up longer. Again and again I insisted they follow my rules, without much success.

Then one day a little book, *The Prophet*, came to my hands, and a lightbulb of illumination went on. I was deeply touched by the chapter "Children," in which Kahlil Gibran affirms "our children don't belong to us. They are sons and daughters of life's longing for itself . . . You may strive to be like them, but seek not to make them like you." The words spoke to my real, authentic self, beyond my own conditioning. At first I fought the idea, hanging onto the belief that I needed to shape my kids into little versions of myself, but because something real had been awakened, little by little it sank in until I embraced it.

Something new and profound emerged from that reading: respect for my kids' unique humanity. And this changed forever the way I related to them. I had always loved my kids, but now I had a new appreciation for them and saw them as complete and unique beings in small bodies. Respect was the missing ingredient in our relationship. After adding it in, I no longer saw them as my property or extensions of myself. Life and Spirit put them under my care for nurturing, to allow them to flourish into the unique person each one came to be—not to twist them and try to make them like me.

Rules like bedtime eventually became more flexible, because I began to listen to their wants and needs. Five-year-old Verónica shared a room with thirteen-year-old Nere. When Verónica was reminded that it was her time to go to bed, with a sad face she usually asked, "Solita?" ("Alone?") I noticed how important it was for her to go with someone, and so I began to take her to bed or make sure her sister was with her.

Opening myself to respect my children was huge. By extension, I began to realize that every human being deserved respect. This changed the way I related to people in general. I hadn't realized how judgmental I had been before, when I was looking at people through the lens of my own myopic experience. I began extending respect to everyone independent of their education or social or economic status, considering everyone an equal, beyond personal or cultural differences.

As the interest in respecting others grew inside of me, so did my ability to listen to others, which helped me develop the corollary attributes of respect: tolerance and gentleness. I became a counselor and later, a conflict resolution mediator, drawing from this acquired ability to show my respect to others by listening carefully to them.

As a conflict resolution mediator, I witnessed the miraculous power of being heard by another person, even when the resistance to doing so was strong.

I recall one holiday season when I was assigned to mediate between a mom and her teenage daughter. They had serious disagreements and no longer spoke to one another. The mom asked for the mediation. The girl was aloof and silent, clearly showing it was not her choice to be there.

There are ground rules in mediation. Both sides agree to treat each other with basic respect, never insulting or calling names. Then each one takes turns speaking about where they stand on the issue of dispute, with no interruptions. When the first person is finished, the other side listens carefully and repeats what they hear until the person who spoke says it was accurate. Then, the other person speaks and the first person must repeat what he/she hears to the satisfaction of the speaker. For a successful mediation process, it is fundamental to listen carefully and ensure that each person is well understood. This is essential to forge a pathway to return to peace.

In my opening remarks, I said to the girl, "I know you have been forced to attend, but, beginning now, you are free to stay or leave. If you stay, there is a big chance for you to be totally heard by your mom, maybe for the first time. That could improve your life."

She decided to stay. We had a long mediation. The mom's big complaint was that her daughter didn't follow her rules while receiving all the benefits of the household. The daughter felt her opinion was never asked nor welcomed and decisions, such as curfew, were rigidly imposed on her. And so, she did not follow them. They spoke and listened to each other as agreed, eventually looking into each other's eyes instead of looking at me, as they had at first. By the end, we created a mutually agreed upon document on how to improve their communication, which they eagerly signed.

They walked out to the parking lot in a lively conversation, visibly enjoying their newfound understanding. As I watched them leaving I could see their loving connection. I felt touched and honored to have witnessed their coming back together.

Listening attentively is one of the most potent forces for change and one of the most valuable gifts we can give to others and to ourselves. We don't need to be counselors or mediators to use it effectively. We only need to be caring, respectful human beings, ready to give our time and full attention to another person. There is a reward after truly listening and giving someone our full attention: an inner satisfaction and fulfillment of having participated in a meaningful way to change the life of another for the better.

Invitation

1. Every person deserves respect simply because they are human.

2. An attitude of respect goes hand in hand with inner peace. When we respect and appreciate the lives of others, we create a space where each of us can express our uniqueness.

3. Respect implies assuming the best intentions of people.

4. Respect could be the missing ingredient in a relationship to make it accepting and peaceful.

5. Listen carefully and try to honestly understand another's point of view. This is a good first step to showing respect and forging a pathway to peace; it is one of the most potent forces for change.

Chapter 6

Living in the Moment

To live in the moment is to focus on what is going on right now rather than on a story in our head from yesterday or what we think may happen tomorrow. I have discovered on my journey that staying in the now is fundamental to being at peace with myself.

We can enjoy happy memories from the past or sweet hopeful dreams for the future, but we must be diligent and careful to notice that there is a strong tendency of the mind to want to modify life. When we turn our thoughts to the past, for instance, our mind often adds a critical observation like: *If only I (or he or she) had not done x, y, or z, then life would have been better.* Those regrets spoil the memory, making us suffer for something we cannot change. In moments like that we can pause, take a deep breath, accept what happened without ifs, and forgive ourselves or the other people involved if necessary. We are evolving beings that keep learning, and as time passes "we do things better because now we know better," as Maya Angelou said. Similarly, when thinking about the future, our minds may have a tendency to worry. "What if I don't get the job?" or "Will I be healthy next year?" Our energy is better spent being intentional about our self-care. Taking care of our health now helps us enjoy a healthy future. Doing our best today empowers us.

Our inclination to regret things that already happened and to fear what might happen brings conflict and discontent—the very opposite of peace.

The good news is that there is another way of living—allowing ourselves to fully connect to the present moment. Experiencing tranquility and contentment in the moment is available to all of us.

In my childhood, my father first showed me how fundamental it was to live in the present instead of hanging on to stories from the past or projecting future hopes to bring happiness.

In 1945, when I was eight years old, my family and I moved to Venezuela to join my dad, who had emigrated from the Basque Country five years earlier to escape the Franco dictatorship and support us. Soon after arriving, my family and numerous exiled Basque families living in Caracas decided to create a community organization called the Basque Center to keep our culture alive.

The Basque community shared the belief that the Franco dictatorship would not last and living in Venezuela would be temporary. As soon as Franco was thrown out, we would return to the old country. The unsaid implication of this belief was that we would not be completely satisfied or happy until that happened. In other words, we lived waiting for the conditions to change.

Dad, however, went against the grain. He insisted we live as permanent residents of Venezuela, believing it was mentally unhealthy to live as temporary sojourners. Dad supported our engagement in the Venezuelan culture instead of living with an eye on returning to the Basque Country. His approach was quite different from many of our Basque friends. Like them, we also spent weekends and holidays at the Basque Center, especially at the beginning, and kept the culture alive in our community. But the emphasis at home was on our adaptation to Venezuela, to our day in, day out reality, our present.

At dinnertime, when the four of us spent time together, usually the conversation began with a cheerful question from Dad to my sister and me: "Hey girls, what happened at school today?" We did not talk about the horrors of the Franco regime or the trauma our dad had gone through. We didn't talk about when or if we would be able to return. Instead, we engaged in what was in front of us, opening ourselves to appreciate the Venezuelan culture, its people, the food and tropical fruits, like mangoes, which were all quite different from the ones we knew in the Basque Country. Dad's approach allowed us to enjoy the many benefits Venezuela and its people offered with less resistance or comparison. He encouraged us to make friends at school, allowing us to adapt easier and faster to our new culture. Mom also focused on the present. She said and wrote to family and friends in the old country what became her coined phrase: "Caracas—primavera perpetua," which translates to "Caracas—perpetual springtime." She modeled for us how to focus on the pleasant weather and fresh flowers at our new home all year around, a relief from the cold winters in the old country.

There is value in preserving the old and known, which we also did in our way. We still enjoy some Basque traditions such as having *turrón* (nougat) at Christmas celebrations. But I appreciate Dad's way to face, accept, and embrace change, the one factor in life that is constant.

He taught us to live in the present and not dwell in the hopes of a different future or the pains of the past, which for him were many. In the Basque Country, he had been incarcerated and almost executed for his political beliefs, then stripped of his pharmacy and his title, forced to start anew across the Atlantic in Venezuela, on a totally unknown continent. By not dwelling on these events, Dad was able to be happy and present for us and we all got to enjoy exploring a new life together. He taught us, not by words but by example. Dad's approach has greatly influenced the way I handle changes in my own life, and made it easier to move and adjust to the USA many years later.

As it turned out, Franco stayed in power for thirty more years, until 1975, when he died of old age. I'm so grateful that our family didn't waste thirty years living for a *possible* future and miss out on the opportunity to actively participate in the life and culture in front of us every day. Embracing change is a fundamental part of living a happy, fulfilled life.

Twelve years ago, in my early seventies, I participated in the Threshold Choir in San Diego, where we sang at the bedside of people who were dying, bringing them ease, comfort, and presence. One day, after five of us finished singing from room to room at the San Diego Hospice, we were immersed in the common joy the singing brought us. I turned to my fellow chorister Barbara and said with a sigh, "I wonder how my transition will be." Her answer was, "Very simple, Nere. You will pass away in the same way you live your life." Wise words. I agree: Living a harmonious, peaceful life is an effective way of having a peaceful passing.

The present is the gift, bringing us joy, peace, and fulfillment. Living fully in each moment, facing what is in front of us, and making the best decisions will create our whole life experience, allowing us to become the author of our own lives, as we are meant to be.

Now is all that we have and all we will ever have. Now is the only moment that exists.

Invitation

1. Life is more enjoyable and engaging when you participate in what is immediately in front of you.

2. A person who is not dwelling on past pain is available for those around him or her.

3. Live for today. Living for an imagined future that may or may not come is a distraction that takes precious time away from actively being engaged in life.

4. Regrets from the past or fear of the future can bring suffering.

5. Change is inevitable. Let's embrace it as quickly as we can so we are able to focus on what is current, the now.

6. Living in the moment means paying attention to what is happening now instead of living in a story of the past or a hope for the future.

Chapter 7

Persistence

In a time when most of us look for instant gratification and immediate results, persistence is not a quality many people value, but it is fundamental in obtaining our heart's desires—for it is in overcoming challenges with focus and diligence that we learn our own capabilities. When, through persistence, we overcome great obstacles and accomplish our goals, we experience peace, and a deep contentment within ourselves pervades.

Let's look at this quality of persistence. We wouldn't need it if there was no impulse to quit. In the face of this we must ask ourselves: What is drawing me to want to quit? We must challenge ourselves to get clear on why the original goal was important and consider if it still is.

Second, we need to look at the obstacles, for without obstacles we wouldn't be inhibited from achieving our goal. Once we are clear that our original goal is still important to us, we need to slow down, reflect, and ask ourselves, are these "obstacles" real? My experience has been that, more often than not, obstacles are tied to some underlying conditioning or assumption. This is what we need to investigate: Is there an underlying belief that is no longer true or no longer serves us? We must remain open to finding fresh solutions to age-old problems.

Persistence teaches us to trust our inner understanding of what we truly want or what is in our highest interest. Being in alignment with our highest aspirations brings us to a place of inner peace and deep contentment.

As with other qualities, some people, like me, have a natural inclination to persist while others must begin from scratch. Maybe because I am a child of war and emigration, persistence is ingrained in me because it was necessary for survival. But no matter where or how you began, life gives us lots of opportunities to practice and improve.

Persistence is helpful, for instance, if we want to follow a new exercise regimen or dietary restrictions. Six months ago, my doctor noticed I had put on ten pounds since my last visit. This alarmed both him and me. Prioritizing my health, and ready to reverse my dangerous weight trend, I changed my diet to salad for lunch, minimized the fat I used in cooking my dinners, and eliminated dessert. I have been persistent with my new diet with good results in my weight loss. I make some exceptions during the holidays, eating some *hallacas* and *turrones*, delicious holiday treats from my Venezuelan and Basque traditions, but I get back on track after the pause. Sometimes a pause is necessary to recharge and be ready to continue.

Although I have had a tendency to persist through difficult challenges, I began to truly appreciate the importance of persistence when I moved to San Diego in 1978. I wanted to pursue a PhD in human behavior and leadership at USIU. I had recently discovered this field and was excited to dig deeper. It touched my heart and fulfilled me in a way I had never felt in the field of economics, which I had studied, worked in, and taught for the previous twenty years. During the previous two years in Venezuela, I had explored the field and noticed the difference it made in my life as well as in the lives of people around me. I was eager to enrich my life with knowledge in an area of great meaning to me and then make it my new line of work.

The initial plan was to complete my degree in three years, the length of my fellowship with Conicit, a research institute in Venezuela that provided financial assistance to me so I could support my family while I was in school.

But, as often happens, at the end of those three years, I needed extra time. I had completed the twenty courses required for the PhD, but my first attempt at the dissertation didn't fly. I needed substantially more time to begin working on a new research topic.

This was overwhelming on many fronts. I felt like I had a choice: to get a full-time job to support my family and myself, or finish my PhD. My first impulse was to quit the PhD and return to Venezuela with the kids. Doing so, however, had a heavy price, literally and figuratively. I would be breaking my contract with Conicit, and I would need to return all the money they had sent for the previous three years, money I didn't have. And more importantly, I would be giving up on my goal to work in this new field that I valued and which fulfilled me. Even though my initial impulse was to quit, when I took a close look, I knew I would be sabotaging myself from the possibility of working in a field I was passionate about.

I would have to live with that.

But I knew that if I rolled up my sleeves and got back to the hard work of finding a new research topic, completing my dissertation, and receiving a PhD, it would ease my return to Venezuela, as it would provide the credentials I needed to work in this new field. Financially, I would be supporting, not hindering, my family. Emotionally, I would be supporting and not hindering myself.

In my heart I knew this, but in front of me I saw insurmountable obstacles. Who would care for the kids? How would I support us?

I had to dig deep, going well beyond my conditioning. The biggest hurdle by far were my kids. It was three years after my divorce, and my conditioning was telling me that I couldn't entrust the care of my precious kids to their father, somehow extending the idea that a failed husband equals a bad father. I had to ask myself if that was true.

I prided myself on being a capable, loving single mother, and their most reliable caregiver. Could I feel confident to turn the main care of the kids over to their father, who had expressed an interest in full-time parenting for a while?

When I thought about it carefully, I had to admit that for the last three years and immediately after our divorce, my ex had diligently co-parented our kids, helping them to adapt to the USA and making their time in San Diego enjoyable. In fact, he was a good father. It was difficult to admit this, but it was the truth.

I realized I had to practice what I had learned and prioritize peace, securing a solution that benefited all of us and met all of our needs. If obtaining this PhD was in all our highest interest, I would persist in following it through and accept that my kids would be fine without me for a while.

I talked to my ex-husband, then to my sister and mom in Venezuela, and finally I talked to the kids. To my surprise, the three youngest were game and in fact looked forward to returning to Venezuela to be under the care of their father and close to their grandmothers, aunts, and cousins. The two oldest wanted to stay in the USA to pursue their education. In short, I was encouraged by all concerned to go forward and complete my PhD.

Persistence was the underlying quality I had to rely on to obtain that degree. I knew the obstacles I faced were big ones and that it seemed easier to quit than to go on. I had to dive not only into the hard work itself, but into the obstacles that faced me and my entire family. A deep sense of peace followed—as if together we had accomplished something worthwhile. My ex-husband got a chance to be the primary parent for a while, the younger kids got a chance to move back to Venezuela and be surrounded by extended family, and the older kids felt empowered and strong staying in the USA.

I learned from that experience that persistence is a valuable tool toward sustainable peace, and I have continued using it to pursue my highest aspirations.

It took persistence to face and overcome more conditioning that kept me attached to receiving a monthly salary for my work. Instead, I took a leap of faith and initiated my own business as a rebirthing practitioner, and continued my training with the World Healing Center, where I eventually was hired and co-led their signature Six Month Intense Program. I needed to step away from the sense of security a salary provided and embark on a practice that would support me differently. It was scary to depend on building a clientele to cover my bills, but I took the risk and persisted. That experience, it turned out, was critically important to the creation of my own practice and healing center in Caracas after my return.

Invitation

1. When the first impulse is to quit, pause and consider the consequences.

2. Get clear and remember *why* reaching the goal is important. Remember what compelled you to reach for the goal in the first place. Acknowledge that life's challenges often require us to make fundamental changes.

3. Give yourself an opportunity to slow down and ponder what is happening. Reflect and investigate what the perceived obstacles are in reaching the goal. Take a look to see if there are conditioned beliefs that no longer serve you.

4. Be open to fresh solutions that can arise when a prior conditioned belief is released.

Chapter 8

Enthusiasm

E nthusiasm is that excitement we feel when we express our passion in pursuing what is important to us. Enthusiasm is a sign that we are following our heart's inclinations, which gives us a feeling of fulfillment—a deep sense of peace and alignment with our authentic selves.

Enthusiasm can be applied to work, hobbies, sports, art, music—the whole spectrum of human expression.

Tuning in to our inherent enthusiasm is an important tool to develop. We need to check in with ourselves and honestly evaluate our enthusiasm. Are we engaged? Happy? Fulfilled? When we can answer yes to each of those, what also comes is a natural feeling of peace and contentment. When we do not feel enthusiastic, it's time to stop and investigate. It is natural for our heart's desire to change. Maybe what once motivated us has waned. There is a tendency to try to hang on to what we once had passion and enthusiasm for, but enthusiasm is more like a river. We need to pay attention to how and where it is flowing or stopped and allow the course of the river of enthusiasm to change. When we follow our inherent enthusiasm, life flows with vitality and inner peace.

I learned to appreciate how enthusiasm manifests in me in the last half of my life. For five years in San Diego, starting in 1980, I received the healing effects of breathwork and the teachings of *A Course in Miracles*. That profound experience propelled me to become a healer using those modalities. I felt it was the most rewarding way to use my innate and acquired talents and support others in what I found so valuable: finding that inner tranquility, that inner peace that makes it possible to enjoy life. With passion, I worked in that field for ten years, three years in the USA and seven more in Venezuela, where I created my own healing center and trained others in the healing modality. During this time I had to persist through different challenges, but I was enthusiastic about my profession. I gave the best of myself in that endeavor. During the tenth year, however, I reached a plateau and felt tired. It surprised me that my interest began to decline until one day I realized my contribution was complete in that area, and I needed to accept it as my personal reality.

It was difficult for me to accept this; it contradicted my assumption that my enthusiasm for that line of work would always stay with me. I was scared that losing it meant I was going backward instead of forward in my evolution. I also feared I would never feel as excited to pursue anything else worthwhile to me in the future. At the time, I didn't know my enthusiasm could be rekindled by something else. Scared, I felt I had lost something meaningful, never to be replaced. *What am I going to do without the excitement I feel for my work, without the sense of joy, reward, and accomplishment for contributing to the well-being of others?* I asked myself.

After a pause that felt like an eternity, what came to me was that my future was in the USA. I felt without a shadow of a doubt that I should move back, this time not temporarily to further my education as I had already done twice, but for good. A new adventure opened up with many possibilities.

With enthusiasm, I embarked on my transition to the USA. First, I needed to complete my work at my center in Venezuela, looking for and finding the right people to continue the work I began. Then, I needed to prepare for the upcoming, multifaceted international move.

At that point I did not understand that, as time goes by, our interests in life change. I needed to allow room within myself to accept and respond to those changes. I needed to be willing to experience a period without enthusiasm. That's scary, but we can take some comfort in observing nature, which comfortably rests during the winter in order to support new growth in spring.

The thing is, what at one moment may excite us doesn't necessarily excite us forever. We are each here to live our unique lives. By observing and paying attention to ourselves without being critical we can continue on the path meant for us. What I learned is that I operate in cycles, and when a cycle is complete, it is time for me to accept it and move on. Later, observing other people's paths, I realize it is a generalized pattern among humans, but nevertheless, it is not easy to accept without questioning. Doubts about our self-worth and creativity can come up and disturb us. Accepting that our life's work may change can help make the pause between projects a time to relax and replenish our energies.

Later on in the USA I became interested in a variety of activities. For example, I became an activist to create a Department of Peace at the federal government level. With all of my passion, I was deeply involved for a couple of years, with great results. (More about this later in the book.) Then, again, I approached a plateau, and my interest began to wane. I needed to accept that I was done with that activity too. By then, I understood my pattern. I stayed calm between involvements, even taking time to let other people involved in the project know of my decision and share how grateful I was to each person and how they enhanced my life.

I had learned to be patient with myself, accepting the end and trusting the next involvement would show up at the right moment after the necessary pause, and that I would approach it with renewed enthusiasm.

In the last chapter on persistence, I talked about facing our impulse to quit. We need to face this impulse and inquire within whether our waning enthusiasm is because there is an obstacle we need to overcome or something else is at play. You might go through the steps outlined in the persistence chapter first. If you convince yourself your highest interest has changed, then it's time to accept the possible discomfort of the pause and move on.

The gap between projects can be unnerving. We may be afraid that our enthusiasm will never return. It's here that we need to relax and trust in our own inherent ability to feel excited about something. We might practice taking baby steps and follow any impulse of vitality, such as riding a bicycle, watching the ocean waves, or taking walks to appreciate the scenery. It's an exercise in trust—sitting in uncertainty, and we can teach ourselves to trust that passion and enthusiasm will return when we follow our heart's desires.

Looking back now, I see that in the last forty years I fulfilled my life's purpose in many ways and with great enthusiasm; what changed was the form of my involvement. My current project is the completion of this book, which I am undertaking with joy, enthusiasm, and persistence. It's my way of extending what I have learned and encouraging all my brothers and sisters to walk the peaceful path.

Each of my projects has provided a specific way to keep me learning, continuing my healing and transformation and contributing to build peace, whether inner, interpersonal, or among communities and nations.

Invitation

1. Check in on your natural enthusiasm and ask yourself these questions: Am I following my heart's desires? Am I excited about my current life's pursuit? Am I engaged? Happy? Fulfilled? If the answer is no, then we must pause and look deeper, inquiring further into the nature of the discontent.

2. Sometimes we reach a plateau and the interest in our involvement declines. When that happens, it's good to check in with ourselves, and consider 1) whether we need to address an obstacle (refer back to the persistence chapter), or 2) whether we feel our contribution in a particular arena is complete.

3. If we realize that our natural enthusiasm has declined because our contribution is complete, it is helpful to accept the inevitable pause between projects as a needed break, trusting the next involvement will show up at the right moment and that we will approach it with renewed enthusiasm. We are not broken if we are not enthusiastic. On the contrary, we may be resting and collecting the energy needed to birth something new—like nature in wintertime.

4. When we embrace and pay attention to following the river of our own enthusiasm, accepting that our interests change, we honor our own unique path and this brings us to peace knowing we have lived with intention and vitality.

Photo Gallery

My son Ignacio Piñerúa had the idea of including pictures in the book. Diligently, he found the appropriate ones and worked with me to make the final choices. I am grateful for your idea, expertise, and dedication, dear Igna.

1944: Seven-year-old me, with older sister Rosa Mari, Grandpa Juan, and Mom, after folkloric dancing at the plaza in our little town Galdakao.

1950: In Venezuela, still catching up with Dad after five years of being apart. Image is blurry, but the love is real.

2004: Involved in the Creation of the Department of Peace at the Federal Level

At the office of our representative, asking for her endorsement of the bill. The presence of my daughter Verónica and my two granddaughters made the visit extra special.

Attending a Susan Davis event at the park.

My granddaughters Viviana and Valeria after a peace parade in San Diego.

2008: Pilgrimage to the Basque Country

With my children and grandkids, visiting my Basque cousins.

Morning fun with my kids and grandkids.

With my five kids in my hometown Galdakao.

2011: Visiting Venezuela with My California Family

Celebrating my 75th birthday in Caracas with friends and family from my three cultures.

On top of the world in Canaima with my kids and grandkids.

After a long expedition to Angel Falls, we settled into our sleeping quarters for the night.

2013: Getting loose on my 77th birthday

2020: The stones with the one word intention for 2021 for each member of the family.

2021: Summer Vacation in Mexico

My adorable grandkids, enjoying each other's company.

Are we having fun yet? The whole gang relaxing in the pool.

Part 3

Living From Abiding Peace

"A life unexamined is not worth living."

—SOCRATES

U p to this point, dear reader, we have taken a look at the importance of setting our intention to live in peace and then orienting our lives toward certain qualities that assist us in keeping and enhancing our intention to live in peace. We've talked about the fundamental nature of forgiveness on the path to living in peace, and considered other complementary qualities: kindness, gratitude, respect, living in the moment, persistence, and enthusiasm.

Now, let's take a look at some obstacles that frequently come along in life which keep us from living in peace.

Obstacles that commonly interfere with our experience of peace include conflicts that arise within our own self (inner conflicts), those that arise in our relations with others (interpersonal conflicts), and those that come from the world around us (external conflicts).

Together, we will find ways to overcome them and be able to return to a place of inner peace.

Chapter 9

Overcoming Inner Conflicts

"When inner conflict ends, peace begins."
—ATTRIBUTED TO BUDDHA

Inner conflicts often spring from discontent and dissatisfaction with our lives, a sure sign we are not following our hearts. It could be we are not aligned with the purpose of our life, or we are not true in our relationships with family, coworkers, or friends. In other words, at some level, we may be lying to ourselves—pretending to be a different person than we are. Old conditioning could be the cause of this—the need to please others, for example, or following old beliefs that no longer speak to us. We all carry our own conditioning baggage.

What can we do to free ourselves from inner conflicts? We need to look inside and spend some time assessing our own selves. We need to examine our beliefs and ask ourselves whether they align with our hearts or are outdated. This is a process, but once we begin this journey, we quickly get familiar with it.

Paying attention to times when we feel unfulfilled can lead us to begin earnestly investigating the underlying cause. It's not always straightforward and it will require all those qualities we just talked about, such as forgiving ourselves for ending up on an unfulfilling path, remembering to offer kindness to ourselves as we investigate, taking care to feel gratitude for all the good we embody, and respecting and appreciating our uniqueness. Ultimately, we each need to learn to ask whether we are living an authentic life that aligns with the person we really are.

If we find we are not living an authentic life, then we must be willing to make a change, to release our old ways to make room for something new. Often this requires a close investigation into our conditioned beliefs—those thoughts and opinions we unconsciously adopted while growing up. I call this "unlearning conditioning."

What are we hanging on to because that is what we were taught or once thought was the best, but which no longer serves us?

Oftentimes we are surrounded by people who believe the things we are now questioning. It's not easy to go against the grain. But to live a life of peace, we must be willing to let go of what we have come to identify with. It is an opportunity to reinvent ourselves and free ourselves from outdated beliefs.

One particular kind of conditioning that can be especially difficult to shake is worrying. Worrying can often feel like we are doing something proactive to protect those we love. I invite you to examine that idea closely.

Finally, we must not overlook a different kind of conditioning: our own resistance to being happy—a stubborn habit many of us have developed that may reinforce an uninvestigated idea that we do not deserve to be happy or should not be happy while others are suffering.

At the end of this section, I introduce one of the strongest tools I have come across to combat any form of conditioning. This tool is the use of affirmations. Affirmations can help us live a peaceful life, especially when we are assaulted by worry and other negative thoughts that create inner conflict. I use them daily.

Let's take a closer look at how each of the things contribute to inner conflict (feeling unfulfilled, unlearning ingrained conditioning, unlearning worry, and resistance to being happy) and also look at how the use of affirmations can help us find our way back to inner balance so that we can let go of our resistance, combat old conditioning and unleash happiness—our direct path to peace.

Feeling Unfulfilled

Unhappiness and dissatisfaction are symptoms of unfulfillment, but they are also our teachers. They can propel us on a journey of self-discovery. It is when we align our lives with who we really are that we can relax and focus on doing our best work, letting go of what no longer serves us, whether that is a career, a lifestyle, or another conditioned belief. Letting go helps us make room for something new, real, and supportive.

So it was with me.

In the 1970s, I lived in northeast Venezuela in a small community called Lecherías. I was married with five children, a tenured professor of economics at the local university. Our lovely home sat on the shore of the Caribbean. I lived a privileged life with accomplishments and possessions which I always assumed would make me happy. Yet, I was not; I was miserable. After a busy day full of personal and professional duties, I felt dissatisfied and unfulfilled. These feelings kept growing, becoming unbearable.

I decided to look inside for the real cause of my distress, to find and face what I needed to work on. What would be my reward? Finding my true self—that gold nugget hidden at that time, but which I knew was deep inside wanting to burst out. I knew the answers were inside me; I just needed to bring them to the surface. How? I didn't know. But I was determined to find out.

My quest began slowly by reading self-help books and attending psychological workshops. Carl Rogers' book *On Becoming a Person* opened up a world of unknown possibilities when I imagined "living as a fully functioning person." Living a fulfilled, happy life intrigued and attracted me. I felt encouraged to confront my life's issues, overcoming the trepidation inside of me that maybe I would find something ugly and dark, and I wouldn't be able to handle it.

Later, in 1975, at thirty-eight, I welcomed a sabbatical—that seventh year when a university professor is released from teaching duties to rest and reflect in whatever way they choose. I devoted that year to moving forward with my inner search.

First, I got clear that choosing economics as my career had not come from a personal interest, but because I went along with what other, well-intentioned adults said I should do. However, even though I excelled in the field, my passion was never there.

I dedicated the rest of my sabbatical to taking different courses and discovering more about myself and others. I learned that my real passion was human nature and the richness of interacting and learning from other people. It was a fascinating and transformational year. When it ended, I knew my days as a professor of economics were over.

That realization was both exciting and scary: exciting because I discovered my passion, scary because my personality—even my identity—was heavily tinted by being a successful economist and professor. After some internal debate, I decided to overcome my fears and follow my passion.

Returning to the university after my sabbatical, the first thing I did was inform the dean of my decision not to teach economics anymore. I offered instead to teach an elective class on human behavior which I created out of my recent year's research and tailored to my engineering students' needs. I would facilitate group interaction instead of lecturing. There would be no tests, midterms, or finals. The only requirement would be an essay in which the students shared what they learned. The students would not address me as a professor. Instead, they would call me by my first name, treating me as an equal.

To my surprise, the dean accepted my proposal. And so I embarked on a new and challenging way to relate to students, no longer as an authority but as a facilitator. It was exciting to put into action a way of being I believed was valuable.

My method was successful for all of us, and we learned a lot. As I let go of the old authoritarian way of teaching, I became approachable to the students. We learned from each other. I repeated the course for another semester.

After that, I was ready for my big career move: relocating to San Diego, California, and enrolling as a PhD candidate in the field of human behavior. I would forever leave economics and the successful career I had been involved in for twenty years.

Invitation

1. Pay attention to any persistent dissatisfaction, or lack of fulfillment. These feelings may indicate a need to investigate what is going on inside.

2. Begin investigating what brings you joy. Try out different things; read books and take workshops that interest you. It's fun to see what naturally draws your attention—not because someone else told you or because you think you *should* do it. This is a time to notice what you *want* to do. Taking one step at a time will help point you in a new direction.

3. Follow where your interest leads you. Allow yourself to be transformed by your own passion.

4. Recognize that transforming yourself may require letting go of attachments to old ways and may feel scary at first. It may even require developing a new identity.

5. Remember, it is worth it because living an unfulfilling life will not bring inner peace and contentment. Look for small steps that can take you from who you were to the person you want to become.

Unlearning Conditioning

Conditioning is a limiting habit that dictates responses to life situations from old and unrevised beliefs. Conditioning comes from our culture, religion, family, or a combination of them. We have all been conditioned. Some of the beliefs we form as a result are more rooted than others.

A Course in Miracles says all we need to do to live a happy, authentic life is to unlearn. Through unlearning, we realize that our conditioning is simply learned behavior and nothing more. It may be a habit or a way we react to others. It may be something we learned from our parents or other authority figures we copied when we were children. As children, we don't know there are other ways to relate; we don't realize our reactions are learned and often stem from fear.

As I mentioned in the previous chapter on forgiveness, early in my transformation I spent a great deal of time unlearning my conditioned response of blaming others when I felt unhappy. When I stopped blaming, I was able to accept my reality and assume responsibility for my own life and my happiness.

Assuming total responsibility for my life in the early 1980s was one of the most transformative things I learned to do; at the time, it was also one of the hardest new beliefs to accept and embrace. I was used to playing the victim role with the disastrous result of feeling helpless and disempowered.

When I moved to the USA to start a new life and career in 1978, I met people with different beliefs than me, beliefs that allowed them to live a happy life now. To assume this way of thinking, I needed to shed some outdated views and revise some deeply ingrained religious beliefs.

I grew up being taught there was a God in the sky who perpetually controlled and judged us, that we were born in sin, that we needed to suffer in life to pay for our multiple sins. Life, as taught to me through my religious upbringing, was all about repenting for our multiple sins, and suffering in this lifetime was needed to experience happiness in an afterlife.

The teachings in *A Course in Miracles* helped me investigate my beliefs and ultimately to adopt a new set of beliefs that included a benevolent Spirit, a powerful love energy that is everywhere and also inside of each of us that we can invoke anytime to receive answers to our questions.

Rather than believing humans were born in sin and destined to be riddled with guilt, I came to embrace the idea that all human beings are innocent and born to live a happy life in this lifetime by following our inner guidance.

My new beliefs helped me be more compassionate to myself and others. I saw that as humans, we all make mistakes, both small and big, and the remedy was not to lay on extra layers of guilt but simply to correct them—to acknowledge our mistake and apologize. Guilt prevents us from feeling happy and at peace with life.

Once I saw the power in investigating my conditioned beliefs and letting go of those that did not serve me, I became interested in looking for what other conditioned beliefs might be causing me fear and suffering. It was quite liberating and soothing to realize that suffering was not required.

Invitation

1. Notice when you are experiencing discomfort. Can you trace it to a particular belief?

2. Investigate the underlying belief. Consider if it resounds in you or if it is just comfortably familiar.

3. Think about if you are willing to let go of the beliefs which keep you bound to suffering. Are you open to living a life of peace now even if it means letting go of something you once thought to be true?

Unlearning Worry

"If a problem is fixable, if a situation is such that you
can do something about it, then there is no need
to worry. If it is not fixable, then there is no help in
worrying. There is no benefit in worrying whatsoever."

—DALAI LAMA

One particularly widespread example of conditioning that
causes suffering to many is worrying. When we worry about
a problem, we allow ourselves to become preoccupied with
a particular issue, fixating on it and adding anxiety to our
experience. Sometimes the problem is a real one, but often it
is imagined. We humans entertain "what if" scenarios easily,
imagining all kinds of terrible outcomes.

Worry is an unconscious learned habit. It can reflect the
way your family handled situations when you grew up—a
behavior you naturally copied. It can even be a deeply
ingrained cultural trait. In some cultures worry is seen as a
necessary response to problems. It can be endemic and difficult
to separate out, just like my ingrained religious belief that I
needed to suffer in order to secure a happy afterlife. But if we
want to live a life of peace, we owe it to ourselves to investigate
anything that causes us to suffer. And the fact is, worrying
causes suffering, even when it is clothed in the idea that our
concern is helping or protecting others. In becoming a person
who habitually worries, we may have innocently adopted
certain behaviors and modes of thinking without realizing

there could be another way to handle those situations. We can bring our desire to help and protect someone to the forefront, but derive it from a place of calm and peace, responding to a problem as it arises instead of causing ourselves unneeded anxiety along the way.

I don't expect you to believe me at face value, for this is your journey. I understand that worrying can feel like a necessary component of love and caring. But I invite you to ask yourself. Is worry *needed* to address a situation? Is feeling anxious required? Does worry actually help resolve the issue at hand? What is truly beneficial in finding a resolution?

As a rule of thumb, if a situation makes you feel anxious, take time to reflect and see if there is another way to approach it.

Let's say you worry after you watch the evening news, which keeps you awake every night; your mind keeps repeating the distressing news you watched. Perhaps as a child you lived in a household where every evening the TV was on with the latest news, and your parents worried aloud about what they saw. This was your "normal" way to conclude the day. But by noticing that worrying about the news disturbs your sleep and causes you suffering, you now have an opportunity to ask whether this habit serves you. It might feel overwhelming to change an ingrained habit, but know this: it is fully possible. Our habits should support our happiness and well-being.

Unlike our habits, however, there are situations in life that are not under our control, like the coronavirus pandemic, for example. Nonetheless, to worry and be preoccupied about it, while perfectly natural, does not resolve the problem. Instead it disables and paralyzes our minds.

Instead of worrying, we want to turn our attention inside and discover possible hidden benefits to the external event over which we have no control. In the case of the pandemic, for example, you might discover you have extra time at home to pursue something important to you. For me, this "silver lining" was taking the extra time to complete my book.

Sometimes we cannot change the circumstances, but we can always change our perspective of them. Be patient with yourself; remember learning new habits takes time. If you stumble, extend compassion to yourself, then get up and continue.

It is possible and worthwhile to unlearn conditioned habits or beliefs that cause us to suffer. Letting go of the suffering allows us to return to our primordial goal to live in peace and contentment.

If you are not sure how to change a habit, you can begin observing what others do in a similar situation and even ask them clarifying questions. That is how I started when I was ready to change my old beliefs. You might ask others: What do you do in the evenings to calm down and go to bed in a relaxed, peaceful state of mind? What is a different habit I can adopt to replace the one that disturbs me? It could be reading a light-hearted book before retiring, watching an uplifting movie, or listening to a calming meditation app.

Finally, if you feel completely overwhelmed by circumstances in your life and paralyzed by your conditioning, a good option is to seek professional help. We all need help sometimes. Below are some steps you can actively take the next time you feel worried.

Steps to Overcoming Worry

1. Notice if you feel obsessed about an issue and ruminate on it frequently.

2. Breathe slowly and deeply five or more times to calm yourself. (Repeat whenever you feel agitated.)

3. Affirm to yourself: "There is another way to see this that will make me feel at peace. I open myself up to receive it."

4. Write down the phrase and keep repeating it, especially if the worrying thought assaults you before retiring to bed. Remember to practice deep intentional breathing if you feel particularly agitated.

5. Trust that in keeping yourself open, you will receive the answer, whether it be in the form of a coincidence, an unexpected conversation, a book presented to you, or a clarifying realization.

6. Follow the guidance received.

Invitation

1. Know this: We are all conditioned as a result of living in society. Conditioning is simply learned behaviors that may be detrimental to our well-being at the present moment.

2. Investigate what behaviors and thinking cause you suffering.

3. Ask yourself whether your suffering is tied to a particular thought or belief. If so, consider whether that thought or belief still serves you in some way. What would happen if you let that thought or belief go?

4. Take the suggested steps to unlearn the conditioned thought or belief that no longer serves you and become responsible for your own happiness.

5. Look closely at whether you have a habit of worrying by imagining the worst possible scenarios. Be proactive and take precautions when necessary, but focus on finding solutions, instead of staying stuck on the problem.

6. Replace old conditioned beliefs or habits with new ones that take your focus away from what causes distress and brings you back to peace.

7. Ask yourself whether "worry" is necessary to show your love and consider whether the anxiety that worrying causes might inhibit an effective response to the situation.

Unleashing Happiness

"Happiness, true happiness, is an inner quality. It
is a state of mind. If your mind is at peace, you are
happy. If your mind is at peace, but you have nothing
else, you can be happy. If you have everything the
world can give—pleasure, possessions, power—but
lack peace of mind, you can never be happy."

—DADA VASWANI

We have been talking about unlearning deep-seated
conditioning, including our religious beliefs, but also a
common tendency of the mind to worry. Now I want to talk
about a different kind of conditioning. This has to do with the
concept of happiness—and specifically our resistance to being
happy *now*. This is important because peace and happiness
come hand in hand.

Happiness means different things to different people.
Some people think of happiness as experiencing pleasure, or
feeling ebullient or joyful, and some relate happiness to a job
well done, or the excited feeling that rushes through when you
finally get something you desire.

I'm talking about happiness in a little different way: I am
talking about it as a state of well-being—an underlying feeling
of contentment and ease. Like the quote at the beginning of
this chapter, I am equating happiness to an inner quality
directly related to feeling at peace. Happiness is a state of
well-being that exists in the present moment. It rests in a calm
approval, trusting we are doing fine given the circumstances.

Why is this important? It is important because it gives us a basis from which to understand our feelings of unhappiness.

Most of us say we want to be happy and invest time and effort to achieve it. What is harder to see is how conditioned we can be to delay our happiness. It is common in our society to believe that one's happiness is based on meeting certain conditions. That's the kind of fleeting happiness I referenced above—I'm happy *when* I eat my favorite dessert, or I'll be happy *when* I get a bonus. In this way, we correlate our happiness to something happening in the future. And when we do so, we resist enjoying life, being happy, and feeling at peace right now. And this moment is the only time when life is actually happening.

To enjoy our life consistently, we need to choose happiness, no matter what is happening or missing now or in the future. It is a personal decision, a commitment to finding our happiness *within* the circumstances we are presented with. Dear reader, I know this does not seem easy to do, but let us walk through how to begin making this switch. For now, know this: Sometimes finding our happiness within whatever is going on is as simple as acknowledging we are doing the best we can under the circumstances, as we experience our feelings of the moment, whatever those feelings are. This is the heart of self-compassion. And, by practicing self-compassion, we model for others to accept their reality, and go through whatever they are facing.

What this means is that feeling at peace or "happy" in the moment does not require only ups, rather it requires a deep acceptance of both the ups *and* downs. This is not about forcing ourselves to be in a perpetually joyful state of mind. It's about trusting ourselves to respond from a place of acceptance to the present circumstances.

Let us first dive into the details on how important it is to experience our feelings in the moment, then we will look at some common conditioning around being happy and the tendency to postpone happiness.

Accepting Circumstances and Acknowledging Our Feelings

When we look closer at the reality of life, we can see why happiness seems so distant sometimes. Right now, many of us are struggling. Some have lost loved ones, like the hundreds of thousands of people who have died during the pandemic; others are dealing with life-threatening diseases such as cancer. Some of us are losing loved ones to Alzheimer's or divorce. Still others have lost their homes to wildfires.

These are real and painful circumstances. So, when I talk here about unleashing happiness, it might sound like I am inviting you to bury your head in the sand and turn away from the pain of such circumstances. Actually, I am not.

On our journey to unleashing happiness—to finding the inherent contentment and ease available when we dedicate our lives to peace—it is fundamental to acknowledge and accept our sorrow, our grief, our confusion. Rather than turning away from the pain, we need to embrace it by feeling it. We need to go through the different stages when facing trauma, including shock and denial, anger, and depression.

In order to live a life of peace and happiness, we need to be willing to feel each of these feelings. In any given moment, we may be overcome with deep sorrow. We may feel abandoned and cry. Experiencing those feelings does not mean, however, that we cannot *also*, underneath, feel at peace. Our feelings are part of being human, and to live a full and authentic life means feeling them when they arise. So, instead of fighting our emotions when we feel angry, fearful, deprived, sad, or depressed—we can accept them. We are humans, and we are doing our best when we experience them and are not avoiding the pain through distractions like work or alcohol. It is best to face our troubles and move ahead until we reach the other side of them. In doing that, we allow ourselves to learn from the experience and reap the underlying benefit of acceptance.

So what does unleashing happiness and experiencing inner peace look like in the face of deep grief? It looks like crying and talking about the people we have lost. It looks like expressing our grief as it arises, not burying it and pretending to be "happy" or peaceful. Mourning is healthy. Mourning is the *next best step* to take when your current circumstances bring you deep grief. In mourning, we keep moving until we arrive on the other side.

Grieving and mourning do not seem like something we would consider "happy," yet they are a fundamental part of being human and expressing the love we feel for others. The Persian poet Hafiz says, "The heart is right to cry when even the tiniest drop of love is taken away."

So, dear reader, when faced with difficult circumstances, the best step to unleashing your deepest contentment is to fully accept what is going on. I don't mean that we don't try to improve our life circumstances; I mean that we accept that this is what is happening right now. It is our reality, even as we take the steps to change it.

If we dismiss our feelings they won't go away. They'll get buried inside, causing us further complications and mental and emotional problems in the future. They will linger, keeping us from feeling at peace. Robert Frost synthesizes it this way: "The best way out is always through."

Hand in hand with acceptance, we can help ourselves by being patient and gentle with ourselves, knowing that in living one day at a time we are taking the steps to return to our peace and contentment. That in spite of the intensity of the feelings there is a reason for hope, believing deep in our hearts *this too shall pass*. Calm will come after the storm.

Let us now take a look at our conditioning to postpone our happiness. Many of us tell ourselves: "I cannot be happy while x is happening in my life or in the world. I need to postpone my happiness until my conditions are met." Two of the most common reasons we are inclined to postpone our happiness are feeling unworthy or undeserving of happiness ourselves, and feeling guilty about being happy while others suffer. Let's look at each of these.

Postponing Happiness Due to Feeling Undeserving or Unworthy

In this case, we postpone our happiness when we hold on to an idea that we are not "deserving" or "worthy" of happiness, so we create self-imposed conditions to achieve before we can feel relaxed and content. These could include obtaining a certain level of financial success, or fame, or being in a certain kind of relationship. We overlook that we can be happy and content *along the way.*

Many people experience underlying contentment and ease without financial or other kinds of success. Others, like myself in my late thirties, remain unhappy in spite of financial and professional recognition. It can be helpful to repeat an affirmation. We also can make signs to post and read frequently with the truth of who we are: "I am an innocent child of the Universe. I deserve to be happy now," or "I am willing to see myself as deserving happiness now." In that way, we can overcome our entrenched conditioning. We can embrace happiness as our birthright without delay, because we deserve it now. As lesson 101 of *A Course in Miracles* boldly states: "God's Will for me is perfect happiness."

Postponing Happiness Due to Guilt

In this case, we postpone our happiness because we feel guilty about being happy while others are suffering. We believe we also need to suffer to show that we see and care about other people's burdens. But, if we pause for a moment and really look at this, we can see that adding our suffering to theirs does not unburden their suffering. It just makes us unhappy too and *decreases* our ability to support them. As I like to think of it, if someone falls in a hole, it doesn't help if I fall in the hole, too. Then two of us are in the hole.

It is hard to see people suffering, especially people dear to us.

Having five children, I have had my share of watching them endure different kinds of struggles, including some larger ones like cancer or divorce. It is not easy. I feel sad and concerned for them and wish for a magic wand to take their pain away.

Fortunately for me, my children's most difficult challenges happened many years after my awakening. I'd already had the chance to work on myself and recognize how important it is to keep my own self in balance, while remaining loving and supportive. I was familiar with the idea of disengaging from the drama (staying out of the pit) and refraining from trying to "rescue" others by controlling their actions—a common conditioned response that surfaces when we want to help a loved one. When our loved one does not make a decision to help their situation, we can easily fall into a pit of despair ourselves.

I understand, dear reader, that it may seem difficult to be loving and disengaged at the same time. It may feel impossible to trust the troubled one to make good choices on their own, especially if they have not been doing that for some time. But, I promise you, it is worth it to not rescue them. Stepping back and empowering another when they are at a low point may open a door, a possibility they did not see before. This also at least allows the two of you to not fall into the pit, and remain emotionally stable. Working on ourselves and overcoming our own conditioning, such as the inclination to "rescue" another, is quite rewarding, as it constantly improves the quality of our lives and promotes assisting others to find their own ways, without controlling them.

Out of fairness and respect for all of my five children, I have not included stories about them in this book. Why? Because they are not my stories but theirs, and they have the right to share them or not with whomever they want. My son Enrique agreed for the story about the inheritance to be included in the book, which you will read later.

It may now be overly simple, but one of the most important lessons I have learned is to trust that my loved ones will find their own way. I know that the inner guidance I received is also available to them. And frequently their way surprises me, just as my decisions sometimes don't fit their expectations. Mutually respecting each other's individuality makes it possible to keep us relating to each other harmoniously.

Stepping back and caring for ourselves empowers our loved ones to be in charge of their own lives. Guilt, though common, is unnecessary, as we haven't done anything wrong. Instead, we can acknowledge ourselves for initiating a different way of behavior that leads by example and creates the space for each person to breathe and own their individuality without controlling or being controlled. Not easy, especially at first, but possible.

Our best course of action is to healthfully disengage from the drama, while remaining connected to the essence of the people who are struggling. We want to hold them in their perfection while maintaining our own footing.

What do I mean by that? I mean empower them, imagine and let them know we already visualize them out of the troubled situation and that it is possible and up to them to decide. And that we hope they will decide to do that. That we are there to make it easier, if possible, and also to cheer them on. And that we believe in them, and they have all it takes to come out of the situation successfully.

The first time we do this it is not easy at all. It goes against the way we were used to reacting, but as a new skill we are developing, practice will make next time easier. And by continuing to practice, it can become our new, natural response to drama.

Many times people have loved ones who are struggling with mental illness or addictions, and those loved ones simply do not make the choices necessary to live a healthy life. We cannot force anyone to change, only support them if they choose to change. We have to get clear that regardless of other people's choices, we need to take care of the only person we are responsible for—*ourselves*. We need to choose our own happiness regardless of their choices, without remorse.

Let me emphasize this again: Feeling guilty is not helpful or necessary for anyone. *A Course in Miracles* states that guilt is an invention of the ego, and the only purpose of guilt is to make us suffer. Keep repeating to yourself and modeling for others the truth: "I am innocent. I deserve to be happy now."

Embracing Your Passion

As we talked about in Chapter 2, what this all comes down to is remembering that the present moment is all we have and *now* is the time. From the *now*, everything we want to do begins, and we are more effective when we are happy and at ease than when we are in distress. Why? Because free from suffering, we are not constricted any more, and the liberated energy can be used to pursue our passions with renewed enthusiasm.

I encourage all of us to look for our passion. And once we find it, let's get on with the issues we are passionate about. As a society, we all benefit from that. And it can inspire others to do the same. This is similar to what we talked about in the Fulfillment section. Finding and engaging in my passion through my line of work to support others to live their best possible life was key for me to feel fulfilled and become a happy person. When we engage in activities we are passionate about, the involvement itself brings us peace and contentment. And it has the potential to make others happy too. A win-win.

Interrupting Our Conditioning

There's no question we are conditioned by our society. For instance, as part of a consumer-oriented culture, we are perpetually drawn into the future by the pull to accumulate new things that promise to make us happy. The ongoing marketing message is that I will be happy when I get a bigger house, or when I get a new car. Then, at a future date, I can relax, *then* I can enjoy, *then* I can be happy.

Additionally, we are in a media-driven society that offers a constant invitation to get involved in the drama and violence going on in the world. Watching the news, which is mostly bad news, can be addictive, and can disturb our minds because of our tendency to ruminate on it, distracting us from what is happening in front of us now. It is an invitation to focus on the negative and can cause us great distress and even intrude on our sleep with nightmares.

Of course it is important to be informed, and know what's going on. What I am referring to is the excess, the fixation on the news that can deteriorate the quality of our lives. There is a great saying: "What we focus on expands." When we focus constantly on bad news, negativity increases. We need to begin to pay attention to how we are affected by and how much time we spend listening to bad news.

If we condition ourselves to look out at the world and only see problems, we train ourselves to believe that there is always something wrong with this moment. This creates a perpetual cycle of drama as we become habituated to look for problems. It costs us a lot of time and energy, making us anxious and preoccupied. We never fully relax in the moment.

But there is another way—it involves shifting our focus to our sphere of influence and to our passion. Instead of passively being at the mercy of what others consider news, we can actively become involved in creating our own "news"— positive, beneficial news.

Let's say you take several hours a day to watch morning and evening news, plus a violent horror movie before going to bed. Imagine how much time and energy you might gain if you changed those habits. Many hours a day would be available to pursue your heart's desire, creating your own reality, plus time to relax and enjoy life. I encourage us to take a deeper look at our conditioning and pay attention to how we are spending our time, and ask whether it is in alignment with our heart's desire.

It's all about interrupting our conditioning—conditioning that we may have picked up just from being a member of society, but which has resulted in habits that do not support our well-being.

The good news is, we can interrupt this conditioning and unleash happiness in our lives now. We can investigate what is keeping our happiness at bay. It helps to ask ourselves pointed questions and dive down deeper with each one.

Having lived the first half of my life with many accomplishments and material things that didn't make me fulfilled and happy and the second half pursuing, acquiring, and keeping inner peace, which brought me the happiness I so longed for, I am here to tell you happiness is totally available for any one of us now, without delays. The only condition is: we have to choose it. We are in charge.

Choosing Happiness

I am proposing something big here. I am suggesting that to enjoy our life as a constant we need to *choose* happiness, no matter what is happening or missing now or in the future. It is a personal decision, a commitment to find happiness within the circumstances with which we are presented.

Before I tell you how to go about doing this, know this: I do not mean to devalue the real challenges you might face in life. You may face abuse or unmentionable grief. You may be living in poverty or be estranged from loved ones. You may strive to improve the living conditions for yourself or your family. You may strive to make this world more just. What I am suggesting here is that you allow the possibility that you can find peace and ease *while* you strive to improve the circumstances for yourself, your family, or the world. It's a change of mindset.

So how do we go about this?

You start wherever you are. You start by accepting that whatever difficult conditions happening at the moment are real: Life right now *is* challenging.

Then you acknowledge your feelings for what you are going through, like frustration, sadness, or depression. This immediately allows you to feel validated. It can help to tune into the physical feelings in the body for a moment too. Tuning into the body brings us back to the present moment, away from fearful thoughts of the future or painful memories from the past.

Notice that as soon as you recognize that what you are going through is hard and your feelings are valid, a space opens up. You innately know you are doing the best you can do. This is critical, for it opens the doorway to be at peace even in the middle of great struggle. This can open you to change your mindset from "There is something wrong that must be fixed *before* I can be happy" to "I open myself to feel at ease with what I am going through right now." That can make a difference for the better.

But that shift will require something from you. It will require clear, focused attention and commitment. It will require you to look closely at how you are spending your time and decide whether it is aligned with your goals. It will require you to keep discovering and be grateful for all you *do* have, and to enjoy the process of effective change. You are choosing to be happy right now by accepting life as it is. Acceptance is the key. You are choosing not to withhold that happiness for a later date with different circumstances.

Steps to Unleash Happiness

1. Notice if you feel unhappy, dissatisfied, or disturbed.

2. Breathe slowly and deeply until you calm yourself. (Repeat as needed.)

3. Then, ask yourself directly what you are feeling. Am I afraid? Am I angry? Am I sad? Am I confused or overwhelmed?

4. Acknowledge whatever it is you are feeling. Tell yourself, it is okay to feel afraid, angry, confused, or sad, too. It is part of being human and it too shall pass.

5. Take a moment to notice the actual physical sensations to bring yourself back into your body and what is going on right now. Our stories can run unchecked in our head, but getting in touch with the underlying physical sensations can bring us back into this moment.

6. Be kind with yourself if you are feeling unworthy or guilty or if you have gotten involved in another person's drama. It happens. Acknowledge and validate those feelings too. Accept that at any moment you are doing the best you can given the current circumstances, and tell yourself: "I deserve to be happy right now."

7. Look at how you are spending your time and energy to be sure it is in alignment with your passion. When we actively engage in what we are passionate about, we feel happier.

Invitation

Ask yourself these questions:

1. Do I feel undeserving or unworthy of happiness? Is happiness something that should be tied to my sense of self-worth? Might I embrace happiness in spite of my shortcomings?

2. Do I feel guilty about being happy while others are suffering? Does my distress help others? Or can I help better if I am centered? Do I believe I should wait until others are happy to be happy myself?

3. Am I, in some way, postponing my happiness for a specific event in the future? Do I believe I need to be suffering in order to be effective?

4. Can I let go of my conditioning to embrace my happiness now? What's in the way of my being happy, regardless of circumstances?

5. What am I passionate about? What is my heart's desire? Is the use of my time aligned with my passion? Are there adjustments I could make to free up more time and energy?

Affirmations

"When you focus on the good, the good gets better."

—ABRAHAM HICKS

I learned the use of affirmations as a tool for reprogramming my mind way back in the eighties when, devoted to my personal transformation, I got involved with rebirthing. At that time I began to use a simple affirmation:

"I, Nere, deserve to be loved."

This was fundamental in helping me change my opinion of myself and initiated me on my peaceful path.

An affirmation is an assertion that something exists or is true. Rebirthing uses affirmations to reverse old hurting beliefs, many of them related to early childhood or birth trauma. They come to the surface while breathing deeply for a while. At first, it is difficult to accept the affirmations because the opposing old beliefs are so ingrained in us. But if we keep writing and reading them patiently, they will sink into our minds and become our new beliefs. Repetition is the key to success. As children we learned through repetition, listening again and again to what our loved ones told us. This works for adults, too, and we can use it as a technique to implant positive assertions about ourselves.

Frequently, we are traumatized by how we were treated as children. Growing up, we may have heard the adults in our lives telling us again and again, "You are stupid," or "You are worthless," or something similar. With the openness and natural trust of children, we believe these phrases as true statements of who we are. After constantly being referred to in those terms, we begin seeing ourselves as stupid or worthless and carry this burden into adulthood, making it extra difficult to succeed in life—first as students, then when relating to others, and later when supporting ourselves.

Even if we weren't specifically traumatized as children at home, part of the socialization process can create feelings of low self-esteem. It can come from comparing ourselves with classmates and deciding that, since we were not similar, our value was unequal. That assumption can be aggravated if we are bullied at school.

When we turn our attention inward and work to overcome our negative conditioning so as to begin to see ourselves differently, we can begin to make gradual change, taking intermediate steps with affirmations.

For instance, if, for whatever reason, we have adopted the belief that "I am stupid," it may feel like too much of a stretch to say "I am smart." The mind could put up a fight arguing all the reasons and "proof" that we're not smart. Instead, it can help to open ourselves up to the possibility of changing our mind by saying an intermediate affirmation:

"I, _____, now open myself up to see that I am intelligent and capable."

This allows our vision of ourselves to gradually expand.

After a while, when the intermediate affirmation has sunk in, you can progress to the final affirmation.

"Now I, _____, see myself as an intelligent and capable person."

Another situation to consider is the fact that many people seem to be moving into negativity. This could be a consequence of the pandemic or other challenging events of the times we live in, including political strife, racism, and the polarization of beliefs. Many have lost family or friends, or their jobs. Many are suffering from anxiety or depression and feeling deprived with the confinement and other changes we have witnessed. The progressive affirmation for people in this kind of situation who are wanting to see the light after the tunnel could include statements like "I, _____, am deserving of _____," "I, _____, am able to open up to a different reality," or "I, _____, am willing to see and embrace all the good people and things in my life. I open up to receive them."

When we open up to see the good in our lives, even while we are suffering, we begin to attune ourselves to small pieces of life we can be grateful for that exist alongside things that cause us pain. It may start with noticing the warmth of the sun or the wildflowers on a field, or appreciating the guy or gal who makes our coffee—anything can catch our attention once we begin to attune ourselves to look for it. You can try this out for yourself.

When you feel stuck, incapable of, or doubting how to help yourself, don't be afraid to reach out and look for professional help. I did it at the beginning of my journey, and it was fundamental to get on track, find myself, and pursue a peaceful, joyful life. You, my dear reader, deserve it. Don't hold back; you are important, and it is time for you to see, accept, and embrace your worthiness. Seeking help is never a bad idea. A simple affirmation to help you move forward might be:

"I, _____, am willing to seek the help I need to end suffering. I deserve to be happy."

Even without a global pandemic adding stress to our normal daily lives, specific circumstances and our own conditioning send us invitations now and then to think negatively, causing us to feel bad about others and ourselves.

Maybe we are driving to work and someone cuts us off. We may feel scared, heart racing suddenly, and think: "That guy cut me off. What a jerk! I could have died." Then we can get angry and feel victimized.

When we notice this, we have a choice: We can succumb and buy into that reaction and ruin the rest of our day. Or, we can invite ourselves to calm down and then gently reflect on other ways to see it.

By looking to the opposite side, to the positive, we can reverse these negative thought patterns and create a specific affirmation that can be repeated again and again, asserting ourselves in our chosen path to live a peaceful, happy life. An affirmation like this reaffirms our new way to see things:

"I, _____, am calm and alert while driving, and my driving experiences from now on reflect it. All is well."

Creating affirmations may feel unreasonable at first—like we are conning ourselves. But it works. The real "con," dear reader, turns out to be all the negative self-talk we pay attention to.

To this day, I use affirmations as a fundamental tool for my personal growth. It is something I intend to keep doing as long as I am alive. And you can do it, too. It is easy and effective.

This is a current favorite affirmation that I repeat daily:

"My joy and happiness increase every day."

It reinforces my intention to become more joyful and happy in all my daily involvement with people and activities.

I also benefit from receiving affirmations from outside sources whose mission, in part, is to aid people on their spiritual journey. For many decades I have received the Daily Word from Unity, a daily affirmative prayer published since 1924 and now available electronically. The Daily Word inspires us to live our best possible lives, or, simply said, "It touches the hearts and minds of readers wherever they are in their spiritual journey."

The many topics it covers include health, prosperity, detachment, guidance, hope, and of course peace, both personal and global. Each day, the chosen topic begins and ends with an affirmative prayer, like this one about joy:

"Acting from the joy in my heart, I accomplish great things."

Or this one on oneness:

"I live in harmony with a diverse world."

Many times the Daily Word reminds and inspires me to move forward in something I am going through at the moment.

The constant use of affirmations is one of the most valuable tools we can use to keep improving the quality of our thoughts. It helps us to return to or to keep focusing on the positive world we want and deserve to live in.

You can create your own affirmations; it is easy. If you observe a negative thought that comes and bothers you, you can turn it around to benefit you.

For instance, last year one of my children disapproved of something I did, and I was disturbed for the rest of the day. The morning after, refreshed and with a clear mind, I remembered how I craved approval. This affirmation came through:

"Today I, Nere, declare I am whole and complete, made to my Creator's image. Now I give myself the only approval I need, the one from myself."

Reading this affirmation daily has increased my self-confidence and reminded me I am in charge of my own happiness.

Practice creating your own affirmation and you will be rewarded with improved results. You always can ask for help from people you know, too.

Below are some affirmations I have used in my practice. You can try them for yourself. I recommend sticking with an affirmation for several weeks, until you feel it is firmly planted in your mind. It is helpful to establish a ritual for repeating your affirmations at least once a day so it becomes a new habit in your life.

If you regularly drink tea or coffee each morning, for instance, you might decide to read your affirmation(s) during this time.

You might start with the intermediate affirmations that help us begin changing our minds while we are on the path to accept that we deserve to be happy, no matter what.

Some examples of affirmations you can adopt:

- I, _____, deserve to be loved.
- I, _____, am open to seeing things differently.
- My joy and happiness increase every day.
- Intermediate: "I am open to feel more joyful and happy."
- I give myself the only approval I need, one from my own self.
- Intermediate: "I am willing to give myself approval."
- I am calm and at peace.
- Intermediate: "I, _____, deserve to be calm and at peace."
- I, _____, am open and receptive to infinite abundance.
- Every atom of my being is invigorated and healed.
- I create my inner reality and transform my outer reality.

- I, _____, give attention, appreciation, and acceptance to everyone.

These are general affirmations that work well for anyone. But when you confront a challenging situation, it is helpful to create your own specific affirmation to counteract it. Below are basic instructions to help you create your own affirmation when you are in the middle of a disturbing moment, turning around the negative thought underneath.

Steps to Create Your Own Affirmations

1. Notice a negative thought that is disturbing you.

2. Pause and observe it. Notice why it causes suffering. Why is this message a problem for you?

3. Ask yourself what you could believe instead that might empower you to come out of your suffering.

4. Write it down, firmly stating that for yourself. Rewrite it maybe more than once, until it is clearly stated.

5. Read it often. The more you repeat it, the more your mind receives it, until it is yours to stay.

Example

1. Negative thought: I want my loved ones to approve of me.

2. Problem: This is out of my control and leaves me suffering.

3. Issue: I don't want to suffer.

4. Intermediate affirmation: I, _____, am open to seeing myself as whole and complete and am willing to give myself the approval I crave. (To open up to change.)

5. Final affirmation: Today I, Nere, declare I am whole and complete, made in my Creator's image. Now I give myself the only approval I need, one from my own self. (The way you really want to feel about yourself.)

As human beings, sometimes we are tempted to look for the negative. I know; it has happened to me. A leading guidance that helped me keep strengthening my focus on the positive is encapsulated in this quote from *A Course in Miracles:*

"If I am looking for the positive, I won't notice the negative. If I am looking for the negative, I won't notice the positive. The vision of one world will cost you the vision of the other."

This quote is a constant reminder to look for the positive and focus on what works and what is aligned with our true nature and commitment to live a peaceful and joyous life, beyond any invitation to the contrary.

Finally, I want to mention the affirmative prayer, a paragraph or two where we state how we want to handle a situation we are going through. I went through a challenging time five years ago, and here is the affirmative prayer I read daily with good results:

I, Nere, keep myself calm and serene in the face of any and all misunderstandings, financial and otherwise. I breathe deeply, knowing I can always clarify any situation from a place of love and oneness. I remind myself that love is always the answer.

Invitation

1. Pay attention to your negative thoughts. Do they stem from your childhood?

2. How do you think your life will be impacted if you release yourself from these critical voices in your head?

3. Follow the steps above. Start now; you will thank me later.

Chapter 10

Overcoming Interpersonal Conflicts

"People and relationships never stop
being a work in progress."

—NORA ROBERTS

One source of suffering in life can be tied to our
interpersonal relationships. When we are in conflict
with or feel disconnected from a family member, friend, or
boss, our world is disrupted. The impact of being disconnected
or in conflict with someone important to us can range wildly
from resigned acceptance to heart-wrenching anguish. Either
way, we may wish to mend or improve the relationship but
feel stuck in an unhealthy pattern of interaction. Perhaps we
have found that the initiatives to repair the relationship have
been a one-way street with all the work and commitment to
restoration coming only from us. For a resolution to happen,
we need to look for an opening with the other person where

they can accept our invitation and work together. If the openness is absent, the best option is to accept it as the other person's decision and stop insisting.

If we are in the receiving part of a relationship that is toxic, even if the person is important to us, we need to prioritize our well-being and remove ourselves from interacting with them. We might be dealing with an alcoholic or someone with mental health issues. In extreme cases a restraining order may be necessary to protect yourself from harm and the abuser from further legal repercussions.

Setting Boundaries

Often the first place to start in restoring our own inner peace while dealing with some upset in a relationship is to set boundaries. Setting boundaries is important because we signal to ourselves that our own well-being is important. This seems obvious but is often overlooked by people who want to help or please others without including their own well-being in the equation.

One simple example might involve a boss who continually intrudes into our personal time. While we endeavor to do the best job possible, we might find ourselves worn out and desiring uninterrupted time with our family in our free time. We might feel unbalanced yet unsure how to proceed without compromising our job.

In this example, we need to learn to communicate our needs to our boss in a simple, direct, and respectful way: "I need to have undisturbed family time after 6 p.m. every night," or "For my physical health, I need to exercise from 7 to 8 a.m. every morning." Adding, "I like my job, and to give it my best, I need to keep myself balanced." In other words, we need to let others know what our needs are. If we don't, it is fair for them to assume we are doing fine.

Setting boundaries is a huge step in living a peaceful life, for it requires us to honestly assess our needs, to look for areas where we have begun to feel abused and resentful, and to make our own happiness and inner peace a priority.

Setting boundaries is a practical way to be kind to yourself but also can be important to others who might be unaware of the impact of their behavior on you. Setting boundaries is an important first step to improve the mutual understanding of both parties in a relationship.

This can also be a life-saving endeavor if we are suffering from an abusive or toxic relationship. It could be necessary for our own survival to stop interacting with an abusive person, no matter how important they are in our lives.

Even though I had loving, supporting parents-in-law, I have witnessed many abusive parents-in-law who refuse to welcome their in-laws as family but treat them as intruders who disrupt the family balance.

"Suegra," the Spanish word for mother-in-law, has a bad connotation, meaning something like the perpetual poisoner in your intimate relationship—the person who relentlessly criticizes and denigrates you and makes your life difficult and stressful. If that happens to be true for you, talk to your partner about setting boundaries, eliminating invitations to stay at your home or going to theirs, and restricting time together. It is fundamental for the well-being of the abused person and the survival of the marriage.

Setting boundaries is the foundation for restraining orders, when even the courts recognize that a relationship has become so toxic that interaction may lead to harm. We value our own lives, so we stay away. Sometimes, it is necessary for the court to enforce the boundary. In seeking to live a life of peace, we must protect our own well-being. Personal safety always comes first.

Still, I encourage you to keep an open heart. Even within relationships where boundaries were set, there can be an unexpected opening to create a connection with the other person. We might have resigned ourselves to conclude that things are as good as they can get, yet in my experience, I have found that if I stay open and pay attention to opportunities that come along, I will be happily surprised, and my inner peace and life satisfaction can expand.

Invitation

1. Think of someone who asks too much of you, either emotionally or physically.

2. Consider some healthy boundaries you can set to protect yourself, either from exhaustion, frustration, or physical harm.

Redefining Winning

Winning has been defined as a person or group experiencing a victory, usually over another person or group. Somehow it implies someone else has been defeated, there is a winner and a loser, which sounds like a battle.

In the chapter on kindness, we talked about how important it was for me to "win" in discussions and be right early in my life. In my early forties, at the beginning of my awakened life, I needed to unlearn seeing myself on a battlefield with others as my enemies. I began to see others and myself on the same journey toward happiness and fulfillment. I changed my mindset to imagine we were working together, complementing each other, sharing our ideas to gain a better understanding of the topic. I was not *competing* with them but *collaborating* with them. Together, I began to see, we could find a better way to move forward.

Typically, competition is seen as a normal way of behaving in order to reach a goal. With such an attitude, any one person's success comes at the cost of other people. I believed this, too. The result is a restless feeling. Instead of relaxing and enjoying the company of others, I would look for opportunities to demonstrate my abilities to win. In doing so, I kept myself aloof and at arm's length from those I saw as my competitors.

There is an alternative way: working together to achieve a goal. In this way, there are no losers, only collaborators. When we redefine our concept of "winning," we can see that no one has to lose for others to win. A new paradigm opens up: I win when everyone else wins with me.

When I redefined this concept of winning, I was left with a pervasive, peaceful feeling. What a relief! Once I learned that peace came from collaborating instead of competing, I began to apply it in my interactions. I was astounded by the power of working together. Not only did I feel better, more at ease, and connected to others, but together with my fellow collaborators, we were able to achieve great things. Along the way, I also learned that happiness is really about enjoying the process rather than the goal.

The following story is an example of working with others to achieve a goal. It was a big win. It is also a story about enjoying the process along the way—not deferring your happiness or giving up your peace to achieve your goal.

It was September 2003—months after the Iraq invasion—when my dear friend Sunny and I listened to Marianne Williamson's inspirational speech inviting us to become spiritual activists. She talked about a bill introduced two years earlier to the U.S. House of Representatives to create a Department of Peace at a cabinet level. This was already sponsored by many House representatives but needed more support in order to be brought to the floor for discussion. The proposed Department of Peace (DoP) would offer nonviolent solutions to our domestic and international conflicts.

I loved the idea; Sunny did too. My friendship with Sunny was bonded by our common thirst and hunger for peace. Ms. Williamson showed us an avenue to work toward an ambitious possibility to express with words and deeds our passion for a more peaceful world, so we both decided to get involved.

By this time in my journey, I had already learned a lot. Not only was I interested in working on this ambitious Department of Peace project, but I realized it was the perfect moment to use and improve my collaboration skills with no room for competitive egos.

Immediately, Sunny and I began working together on the project. We researched and educated ourselves about the bill to be able to speak about it. We found out we belonged to the 53rd District, and Susan Davis was our representative. We also found four other mature women living in our district who were already individually involved in the initiative. The six of us met and decided to coordinate a plan to work together to ask Susan Davis to endorse the bill. We became very active, taking turns to be present at all of Ms. Davis' public appearances when she was in town, always speaking to her about the bill and asking for her endorsement. We even visited her office in Washington, DC.

As six mature women working jointly, each of us brought our own unique abilities and resources. Working together, we complemented each other and had a much further reach. We visited her staff at her office and distributed information on the bill to lots of people in our district, many of whom decided to back our efforts. Together, we created momentum in San Diego, something Ms. Davis needed to see for her to sign the bill.

It was a well-orchestrated effort.

Our last common task was Saturday, August 14, 2004. In the morning, two of us went to a presentation by Representative Davis at a park, where we passionately asked, implored, and begged her to endorse the bill. Later that afternoon, several of us went to the health fair at the Point Loma Library organized by her staff. Sunny showed up with an exquisite bouquet of two dozen long-stemmed white roses that she presented to Representative Davis at the end of the fair.

Barely two weeks later, the first day in September back at the Capitol after the summer break, Susan Davis endorsed the bill for the Department of Peace. We were elated. In less than a year we had accomplished our ambitious goal.

Unfortunately, after perhaps two more years of work, the bill didn't receive enough endorsements from other districts nationwide to be discussed in the House, and it was dismissed. We didn't reach the common goal of creating a Department of Peace.

I did not feel deflated that the overriding goal was not accomplished. Instead, I appreciated that we were promoting peace at every step along the way—working together, enjoying the process, and pursuing our shared passion.

I greatly enjoyed the process of learning and working closely with five other women on an issue we were passionate about. We recruited many others in our district and together contributed to the 53rd District by expressing support for the bill. Along the way, I did not defer my happiness until such a time that a DoP was formed. I chose to stay happy and at peace as I continued advancing a way to live in a more peaceful world.

Nationally, the effort—though it did not make it all the way through—brought a new vital conversation about the advantages of having a cabinet position exclusively dedicated to advancing peace, internally within our frontiers and externally with other nations. So, together we advanced in our pursuit. It was a *win-win* for the six grandmothers, as we were later called.

You never know how your efforts might affect the world. After the initial DoP vanished, a new, interesting development occurred. Currently, there is a new bill before the House of Representatives introducing a Department of Peacebuilding—a different DoP—with the aim of empowering community peacebuilding, teaching peace in schools, humanizing justice systems, and fostering international peace. Of course, Susan Davis endorsed it.

I hope my descendants will see this bill become law, but first, I hope there is a shift in the mentality of our community to examine and implement nonviolent solutions to such domestic problems as racial discrimination, home violence, and juvenile gangs. Internationally, we need to increase dialogue and negotiations with other countries to bring the sustainable global peace we all want. We need to give peace a chance.

Visit my website, themissingpeacebook.net, for more information on the new DoP, as well as a list of collective initiatives to create and spread peace.

Invitation

Embrace working with others and enjoying the mutual satisfaction of achieving things together. This could be as simple as planning your next vacation with your family where the needs and preferences of all are acknowledged and addressed. Or perhaps you are also an activist. The first step to moving forward is to unlearn outdated, competitive behavior.

The Healing Power of Forgiveness

While setting boundaries can improve a relationship and mending an estranged relationship can be one of the most satisfying endeavors in leading a peaceful life, I also want to talk about forging new relationships where you might never have expected to find one. It's all about staying open to possibility. In Part 2, about the qualities conducive to maintaining peace, I talked about my own story of forgiveness and how it launched me securely on a path to peace. Now, as we investigate interpersonal conflicts, I want to again talk about the healing power of forgiveness and share a dramatic story that underscores the potential of forgiveness to heal a relationship.

"Richard's Forgiveness" is a powerful story that can inspire us when facing our own difficult interpersonal challenges. Hopefully, we will never have to rise to the occasion that Richard did, but it is heartening to know that a relationship can be forged with an enemy, even after a traumatic event.

I heard about this story after returning to San Diego as a permanent resident in 1998. At the time, I rekindled my interest in *A Course in Miracles*. I remembered how *A Course* showed me the way back to peace as I struggled after my divorce. I got in touch with the Miracle Distribution Center and signed up for their bimonthly bulletin. This is where I read about the ongoing story of Richard's forgiveness.

I knew from my own experience twenty years earlier how liberating it was to unburden myself from blaming my ex for the end of our marriage. I could forgive him when I considered his infidelity as a hurtful mistake instead of an action he did to purposefully inflict pain on me. Richard's story was another dimension of the healing possibilities of forgiveness. Richard was able to forgive the perpetrators of his wife's murder, forge a relationship with one of them, and return to peace. I was profoundly touched by his forgiveness process and his powerful healing story.

On May 20, 1987, Michele Molina and Jose Ulivarri invaded the home of Richard (Dick) and Ramona Gayton in La Habra Heights, California, with a gun and a knife, intending to rob them. Ramona Fox Gayton was brutally murdered and Dick's secretary was seriously injured but survived. Dick and his three young children were not home when his wife was killed; he lost his best friend and partner, and their children were left motherless.

Dick was heartbroken—alternating between thoughts of murder and suicide. Daily he faced the agonizing reality of his children missing their mom in many different ways. Every day felt like a nightmare raising his kids.

Michele and José were caught within a week and imprisoned. At Michele and José's sentencing, Dick asked the DA for the death penalty. They were sentenced to life in prison. However, in his everyday misery, while wishing the worst on the perpetrators of the crime, Dick also prayed for ways to heal himself. His brother-in-law gave him a copy of *A Course in Miracles* and as he read about forgiveness, the basic teaching of the book, he internalized how fundamental it could be for him to move on from his misery and achieve the peace of mind he lacked.

He met with other people involved with *A Course* and began to hear a reassuring inner voice of peace that directed him to not only forgive, but to write a book on his forgiveness process. He no longer felt like death was the answer—not for Michele, José, or himself. Slowly he began to write and recover as he continued raising his kids, returned to work as a clinical psychologist, and remarried. Seven years later, in 1994, after finishing his book, *The Forgiving Place: Choosing Peace after Violent Trauma*, he appeared on Oprah. For Dick, forgiveness brought an immediate return to peace after years of painful chaos. He pointed out that his nightmare life dissolved into a quiet joy and a sweet love for the memory of his wife. At the time he thought his forgiveness process was completed.

But in 2001, thirteen years after his wife's murder, the quiet inner voice asked him to contact Michele and José. At first he resisted, but eventually he wrote to them. They both responded. José was clearly mentally ill and dealing with his own demons, but Michele responded with heartfelt apologies, and described the abusive relationship she had endured with

José. She was just nineteen at the time of the crime, already married to José, who punished her when she refused to do what he demanded, even prostituting her. In her fear, she became a puppet in his hands. José had ordered her to be with him at the burglary invasion of the Gaytons' home. He was the perpetrator, but she did not try to stop him.

Michele wanted to make amends in search of her own healing. She wrote to Dick about the spiritual programs she pursued in the California Institute for Women, including teachings from *A Course in Miracles*. She shared her art with him, an important element in her healing. Dick not only forgave her, but he visited her.

Once inside the prison gates, he hugged her. He recognized Michele's healing, and with his forgiveness, she felt even more at peace and wanted to give back to society. She made every attempt at restitution for the survivors of her crime.

Dick decided to seek parole for Michele and testified on her behalf, even though this was bitterly opposed by many friends and relatives, including his then-adult children. With Michele still in prison, Dick went on *The Tyra Banks Show* with one of his adult sons, where they respectfully shared their different positions on the matter. His son did not forgive his mother's murderers, and Dick understood and accepted his son's position.

Around the same time, Michele embarked with Dick on a program to provide *A Course in Miracles* to prisoners around the country.

After twenty-five years in prison, Michele's parole was granted.

In 2014, Michele and Dick appeared together at *A Course in Miracles* International Conference, described as "A unique forgiveness event that has been twenty-five years in the making. Victim and perpetrator will take the stage together for a powerful display of how forgiveness can heal even the most unthinkable act: murder."

On the global public platform, Michele and Dick shared their miracle of forgiveness with the world.

As Dick wrote: "We are all called on to perform extraordinary acts of forgiveness in order to live in joy and peace in this world."

Dick did something extraordinary, way beyond ordinary forgiveness. His reward was extraordinary too; he was able to move beyond his nightmarish life and heal his pain. Forgiveness is a liberation for the person who forgives.

Whether being mistreated or abandoned as a child, discriminated against for our gender or color, or holding onto something silly a partner said, we each often hold grudges against other people. There is nothing wrong with this; it's natural to have a reaction. But ultimately, holding onto a grudge, however big or petty, will not bring us to a state of peace. Why? Because holding a grudge locks us to the past.

We may need to sound the gong of "I have been hurt!" and acknowledge our anger and resentment. And society must actively go after perpetrators of crimes. But if we want to rest in our own inner peace, we need to eventually stop ringing the victim gong and be open to what is available to heal us.

This is not easy or fast. It is much easier to continue our known pattern of anger and blame. But we must continue to check inside and ask ourselves, "Is this working? Do I feel more peaceful and at ease with my life?"

When we realize the answer is no—and there is no particular timeline for forgiveness, only you will know when enough is enough—then, we open ourselves to healing in completely new ways. Even we won't have a clue what this might look and feel like, but we can open ourselves to possibilities and then pay attention to see how they come. Letting go of victimhood, opening in this way, and surrendering to something greater than ourselves is the "little willingness." *A Course in Miracles* says we need for Spirit to intervene and make it possible to forgive. And forgiveness, in turn, releases us from our past victimhood and allows us to resume control of our lives. It also frees the energy we use to hold on to grudges, energy we can use for creative endeavors and moving forward with our lives.

Peace and happiness, joy and creativity, not to mention the potential for forging new relationships, are the rewards.

Invitation

1. Be gentle with yourself. Allow yourself to feel any anger or resentment for having been hurt. Honor your own timeline. Understand that it is important to have your hurt acknowledged.

2. Whenever your well-being is at risk, set healthy boundaries. If your personal safety is threatened, seek the necessary protection from the law.

3. Recognize that maintaining a victim identity may no longer be serving your highest goals.

4. Check in with yourself and ask, is anger, resentment, and the desire to retaliate still working for me? Can I let go of the past and return to live joyously and peacefully now? Am I ready to let go of being a victim?

5. On your journey to healing, allow that it might not happen immediately and don't demand too much from yourself. Instead adopt the attitude from *A Course* to have a "little willingness," an openness for a solution to present itself.

6. Always pay attention and listen for your own loving voice to direct you, as Dick did when he read *A Course in Miracles,* the book on forgiveness that his brother-in-law gave him. Then, consider what additional steps you might take to forge a new relationship.

7. Allow miracles to happen.

Chapter 11

Overcoming External Conflicts

I n Part 3, we have been looking closely at obstacles that may come along in life and challenge us from living in peace. We first talked about conflicts that arise within our own self, "inner conflicts," and looked not only at potential causes, such as feeling unfulfilled in life, but also strategies for overcoming inner conflicts, including unlearning conditioning, unlearning the tendency to worry, unleashing happiness, and using affirmations. Then we took a look at overcoming the conflicts that arise from our relations with others, "interpersonal conflicts." In that chapter, we considered the importance of setting boundaries, how redefining winning can improve interpersonal relations, and we revisited the potential power of forgiveness even when we have been deeply harmed by hearing about an extreme case.

Now, we are going to turn our attention to conflicts that arise from the outside, "external conflicts." We are going to investigate 1) ways to navigate turbulent waters, such as a global pandemic, 2) how to preserve family ties, 3) the art of being proactive, and 4) the impact of money issues as well as the corresponding emotions that can make for a messy external conflict.

Navigating Turbulent Waters

"In the midst of movement and chaos,
keep stillness inside of you."

—DEEPAK CHOPRA

The global coronavirus pandemic was a turbulent time for the whole human race independent of race, gender, social and economic status, or location.

During 2020, extreme measures were taken to avoid the spread of this contagious virus. Public places like restaurants, bars, casinos, and even parks were shut down. Authorities recommended that no more than ten people meet together. Schools were closed. Suggested preventive measures included staying home, keeping a social distance of six feet from others, wearing masks, sanitizing objects of constant use like phones and computers, and refraining from shaking hands or embracing others.

The pandemic touched all of us in different ways, from getting sick or knowing people who have gotten sick or died, to losing a job, to not being able to attend school or having to close your restaurant. Many people's financial well-being was threatened.

As collective fear ran rampant, the stock market plunged. For me, a retired person whose income mostly derives from investments, my financial stability was compromised when my investments lost nearly half of their value in March 2020.

In the face of these critical circumstances, I paused to consider my response to the situation. The events were way beyond my control.

While I knew that I could not control the stock market, I could choose the way I would respond. I could allow fear to possess me and panic, or I could stay calm in spite of it all.

The Universe was screaming, "Are you going to continue applying your lifelong learning from *A Course in Miracles* and keep peace of mind as your number one goal, or are you going to succumb to the pressure of the moment and allow this situation to be in charge and make you miserable?"

In the midst of the crisis, I applied one of my favorite affirmative sayings, the Serenity Prayer. "God, grant me the SERENITY to accept the things I cannot change, the COURAGE to change the things I can, and the WISDOM to know the difference."

I accepted what I couldn't change: the stock market volatility. I changed what I could: my perspective of the situation, choosing peace and calm instead of turmoil and agitation. And, as a practical matter, I became careful with my extra expenses. I took heart in the many people who had influence over the situation and were working hard to alleviate the financial suffering caused by the pandemic.

With my background as an economist, I knew that the nature of the stock market is to fluctuate, and in a situation of collective fear, it can crash. I also knew that historically, in the long run, the stock market recuperates.

The truth is I didn't know when my stocks would recover. As it turns out, they did soon after, and for that I am grateful. I didn't need to look for permanent solutions to cut my expenses drastically, like moving to a cheaper home, or getting a loan, or both. What was clear was that I wouldn't allow money issues to make me anxious and compromise my most precious asset, my inner peace.

When the pandemic came, we all paused, and an important decision surfaced: How do we use this pause? We could go into despair and think, "Oh no, this horrible thing is happening; there is no hope for me or the whole of humanity." Or we could choose another way. After the initial shock, we could take some of the extra time to reflect and come up with a more thoughtful response.

Consider how different it feels to say: "It seems the Universe is talking to the whole human family, asking us to stop and take a break from 'normal.' How can I use this time in the most constructive way possible?" I did not want to be paralyzed by fear, so instead I chose to be open and curious.

We might consider that this pandemic has offered us a natural time to reflect and revisit what our life looked like before and make changes that would empower us.

For the first three months, I didn't go outside my home. However, I still actively searched for the hidden good in the situation. *What can I do with so much extra time at home?* The answer came fast. I decided to use the extra time to complete an exciting project: this book about my peace legacy. The pandemic propelled me to follow my bliss. I knew finding things to be grateful for was key to staying uplifted and at peace. As I embraced this very different "normal," miracles soon began to occur. I noticed an abundance of things for which to be grateful—new and different things I hadn't anticipated or even known were missing.

Phone chats, Facetime, Skype, and Zoom kept me in constant communication with my loved ones, friends, and extended family. I was able to receive and send comfort and support, sharing valuable information, videos, and jokes at a distance.

My financial advisor told me that in spite of the stock market crash, my income would stay the same, so I could pay my bills.

There was an explosion of Zoom classes. I took a six-week class on branding, and discovered what the word meant for a writer. Marni, my writing coach, offered a read and critique class in which I reaped the benefits of seasoned writers listening and giving me valuable feedback to enhance my writing. Both activities aligned with my chosen focus.

In addition, my chair yoga teacher reinvented herself, offering Zoom classes three times a week. And my favorite gold Zumba teacher suddenly began offering online classes twice a week. Both activities allowed me to continue exercising from the convenience of my home.

My son Pascual stayed with me, adding good company and great conversations, plus his help with food shopping, cooking, running errands, and fixing things at home.

What else could I ask for? All fronts were covered, allowing me to enjoy my reclusive, unexpected time out. The generous Universe added to my intention to make this time memorable.

Choosing to make lemonade out of lemons and infusing it with my unique flavor has been my joy. It feels so much better than complaining and cursing the lemons while feeling victimized.

The power is inside each of us and we can decide, from a calm place, to use it to advance our happiness and contentment, rather than feel victimized and miserable. This moment has given us an opportunity to be in charge instead of giving our power to circumstances. Changes are a sure thing in life. The pandemic will pass, but other challenges will show up. Assuming total responsibility for the quality of our lives, we can overcome the ins and outs of the pandemic and any other future challenges, using them to empower us and our surroundings.

On this journey of peace, it helps to have like-minded people around, even if they are only available via Zoom. Though we are isolated, we are embraced mightily by our companions at a distance.

Unprecedented acts of kindness and creative opportunities are happening in this unprecedented time. The internet began offering virtual visits to museums, all kinds of music from classical and operas, dancing classes, reflection and meditation sessions, and many other choices. A famous Venezuelan singer, José Luis Rodríguez, "el Puma," changed the wording of his famous song *Agárrense de las Manos,* "Hold Each Other's Hands," to a supportive one for the times:

"Do not hold each other's hands." In the same fashion, Neil Diamond, in a video from his living room, offered a version of *Sweet Caroline*, encouraging the adoption of the new rules to avoid getting infected. People wanting to help others made "We are in this together" a daily reality.

We won't be the same after having collaborated with the whole world to overcome the virus. The virus crisis has pushed us to evolve as the global family we are, connecting us all as brothers and sisters.

Invitation

1. When facing an unusual circumstance, pause and consider your best response before reacting.

2. Choose calm over fear.

3. Believe that you have the power to change your perspective on any situation. Be open to discover a bright side where initially you saw only darkness.

Preserving Family Ties

While the world at large might bring us broader external conflicts, such as a global pandemic that touched every human on our planet, sometimes our external conflicts stem from something closer to our own heart: our family. In such cases, we must not only think of positive ways to handle complex situations, but also consider ways to communicate kindly and effectively with those who are closest to us but may not share our views. There are ways, too, that we can be proactive to help prevent disagreements among family members.

Inheritance Issues

Emotions run high in families when a loved one is lost. While many families navigate this new terrain with grace, it is also common for survivors to disagree and fight about the inheritance, sometimes dividing families. That is what happened to my father.

As a young man, my father experienced the long-lasting consequence of a dispute over a family inheritance where his siblings divided—two on one side and four on the other—and mostly stopped speaking to the other side for the rest of their lives.

This greatly affected my dad, who took this painful lesson to heart. As a consequence, he made preserving family ties a highest priority. So, twenty-five years later, when his older brother Jesús died, Dad clearly and decisively moved to preserve the family union, even though it required him to let go of his position—and his house.

Some years before, Uncle Jesús and Dad had built their dream homes for their families; the houses were attached to each other. Both families enjoyed living there. When Uncle Jesús died, Dad proposed to buy his part from his heirs, but they didn't accept the proposal. Instead, the heirs were convinced the property should be sold altogether. And Dad, remembering how devastating a rift over an inheritance could be to a family, conceded his position and our home was sold.

I was a college student and wanted to stay in our family home; it was hard for me to accept that an era was ending. Nevertheless, I admit my father planted a seed in me to prioritize family ties over material possessions and money.

That seed had a chance to sprout within me, and forty years later I had the chance to test where my priorities were.

The opportunity showed up when I participated in a complicated inheritance my adult children were involved in after their father (my ex) died. Enrique Sr. and his new family, a wife and two kids, had been living on a family property called El Cocal, a coconut plantation in rural eastern Venezuela. The property had originally been owned by his grandparents, and Enrique Sr. was one of their twenty-five grandchildren, their direct descendants.

When my ex, Enrique Sr., died, everything about the property was up in the air. Without a will specifying what should be done, the common law ruled: the twenty-five grandkids—the direct descendants of the original owners—

jointly and equally owned the property. It took ten years to unravel and solve the complex situation.

The plantation was located in a remote area on the Eastern Caribbean Sea, far away from most of the heirs' urban locations. Many years before, Enrique Sr. moved there when he got a job managing the nearby port. He met his new wife there, and they built their family home on the plantation. None of the other heirs minded, and they enjoyed staying with Enrique Sr. and his family when they visited. My children loved visiting their father at his home there.

When Enrique Sr. died, his one-twenty-fifth portion was passed on to his own eight heirs, his new wife and their two children and my five children.

My son, Enrique Jr., one of the eight heirs of Enrique Sr.'s one-twenty-fifth share, took on the complicated task of resolving the situation. He started by talking to his immediate siblings so that they all would be on the same page to present it to the other twenty-four heirs. But initially he was extremely distraught after his father's sudden death, and his communication skills were compromised. He didn't listen to his siblings' opinions, and tried to impose his point of view on them. Instead of creating a unified plan of action to present to the rest of the heirs, the conversations with his immediate siblings became disputes, where Enrique Jr. tried to push his way to keep the property "no matter what." They screamed and insulted each other, increasing their distance. It was a mess. The discord escalated until the two sides completely stopped communicating.

After almost two years of failing to find common ground, all of my kids were frustrated. They did not know what else to do. I felt deeply saddened and concerned watching my children so divided. Then, the possibility for a solution came to my mind. At the time I was active with the San Diego Conflict Resolution Center, and I found two colleagues willing to mediate for my five children if they agreed to participate.

When I proposed a mediation, they all were relieved. They agreed to participate and dedicated a whole weekend to the mediation under the expertise of two seasoned mediators to find a position that represented the five of them.

Agreeing to mediate created the bridge between them, a signal that all five hoped for an understanding with one another and accepted that they needed help to get there.

After the mediation, little by little, the five of them began mending their broken relationships, returning to the closeness they'd had before their dad had died.

In the signed agreement produced at the mediation, they chose Enrique Jr. to represent and negotiate with the other heirs, without lawyers, under the common terms found in the mediation: to preserve the property as a valuable family vacation destination, not to be sold to a third party. The heirs who wanted to keep the property could buy from those who wanted to sell their portion. Enrique Jr. agreed to report regularly to his siblings on how the negotiations were proceeding. An appraisal of the property was ordered to find its current value, including the substantial improvements

Enrique Sr. added, and these figures were used to negotiate with the other heirs.

Two years after his dad's passing, Enrique Jr. was better emotionally; he was willing to learn and do his best to negotiate with the other heirs. Throughout the mediation with his siblings, he learned how crucial it was to listen attentively to the desires and opinions of others in order to negotiate with them, instead of trying to impose his point of view, which ended in discord. He applied his learnings in his conversations with members of the extended family. Through trial and error, he became a good listener, making it possible to find solutions that suited everyone.

For all of my five kids, El Cocal was a magical place linked with sweet memories related to their father. The property was the point of entrance to Venezuela for their great-grandparents, Sara and Antonio, who emigrated from Lebanon one hundred years earlier, and was a cherished symbol of the family's beginning in the country. The heirs and their families were sentimentally bonded to El Cocal and had fond memories of bathing on its shores while visiting.

When my children were small, their dad took them there every year for a two-week summer vacation. Excited with anticipation, their cousins—my sister's children—joined them. When they arrived, they discarded their shoes and wore the Venezuelan "alpargatas," a rustic and simple footwear, a metaphor for leaving behind school and civilization and embracing their simple vacation, mostly focused on the warm and quiet Caribbean Sea adjacent to the property. A picture I have of four of them riding a donkey illustrates the simple life they enjoyed there.

When Enrique Jr. reinitiated his conversations with the other twenty-four heirs, he trusted I could help him. I became his sounding board at every step. He and I spent hundreds of hours on the phone during those precious eight years. Sometimes he was discouraged, other times excited, but he stayed on course. I listened to him and encouraged him to continue, pause when he needed to reflect, and find the best solution with each successor.

As we worked together, I was excited to have the opportunity to share with Enrique the tools I learned on my journey as a conflict resolution mediator. It became clear to me that we were creating a new family paradigm, adopting my dad's clarity that preserving family ties should always take precedence. I was happy to be able to add some practical communication skills I learned to make it easier to find common ground.

Enrique and I talked about the need to be patient, to listen carefully, and to hold in our hearts that it was possible to find a peaceful agreement with each of the other heirs. We talked about not reacting to any proposal, not taking things personally, but rather allowing some time to reflect.

In his pursuit, Enrique visited Venezuela from his California home, and took the time to talk once and again to each heir to understand what they wanted, which ranged from financial compensation to staying involved as property partners. He addressed many different situations and positions. In his heart, he knew his dad would want him to follow the congenial path to preserve the sacred family ties. That conviction was fundamental to his ability to stay on track for such a long time.

After ten years, the inheritance issue was resolved. Enrique Sr.'s widow and his seven direct descendants kept the vast majority of the property and its administration by buying from the heirs who preferred to sell. Everyone received what they wanted, and family ties strengthened.

Working together in the complicated inheritance issue taught Enrique Jr. and I many lessons. Enrique became a good listener, and now he continues to search for common ground when problems arise in our family's interactions.

We both did not accept the constant invitation of the world's "instant gratification" model pushing us to be in a hurry and act quickly. Many times the best and most valuable solution is not the fastest, especially when matters of the heart are involved. A pause is, at times, the best course of action.

My relationship with my son Enrique also benefited from our working together on this. Focusing on finding the best solution with each heir created a new bond and deep understanding, finding together, again and again, what the next step should be.

The El Cocal inheritance is the longest conflict-resolution project I have ever been involved in and the most rewarding one. The most valuable benefit was that family relations were greatly enhanced. It was a labor of love, and everyone in the family won.

Invitation

1. Have an open mind when you get involved in a complicated situation with others; try not to be attached to your own predetermined position as the best course of action.

2. Recognize that you might be in an emotionally disturbed place that is affecting how you interact with others. Look for help to resolve it.

3. Consider what your highest priorities are. These may no longer align with your initial gut reaction to the issue.

4. If the parties are unable to work out a peaceful resolution, consider the use of a neutral third-party facilitator, such as a mediator, so everyone feels heard and their position is understood.

5. Engage in the process. Be ready to speak what you see as the best path, while also listening for wisdom, truth, or the most compelling proposal, which may come from someone else.

6. Allow yourself to be changed by the process and learn what kind of communication mends discord and what kind of communication makes it worse. It is empowering to collaborate to find an agreement.

7. Be patient. Be persistent. If needed, take a break. Try not to react and if you do, apologize and go back to listening respectfully.

8. Allow the situation to unfold naturally without pressing for a fast resolution. Many times simply allowing more time aids in finding a solution.

9. Create and maintain one-on-one communication instead of delegating the solution to the impersonal legal system.

10. Forgive others and yourself for human mistakes, giving space for reconciliation.

11. Always stay focused on the reward, the amicable resolution. It will give you strength to keep going.

Being Proactive

In this chapter, we have been looking primarily at overcoming external obstacles to our peace. We took a long look at inheritance issues, which can cause stress and separation until they are resolved. I would like to take a moment, now, to talk about the power of being proactive to avoid inheritance-related conflicts for our descendants. It can help us feel at peace, too, knowing that there are no loose ends that our family will need to struggle with during an emotionally charged time for them.

After my mother's passing in 2000, I became aware that, with my parents gone, I was next. I appreciated the clarity my parents had about what they wanted to happen with their possessions after their deaths. They told my sister Rosa Mari and me their wishes, and then they wrote an agreement that the four of us signed. At their passing there were no surprises and the distribution proceeded peacefully.

I wanted to create something along these lines for my kids with my modest inheritance to make it easier for them too and prevent conflict among them after my passing.

I came up with a three-way plan. First, I needed to get clear about what I wanted. Second, I needed to create a legal document reflecting my wishes, and third, I needed to give a copy to each of my children and open up a conversation so the five of them were clear about my decisions and desires.

After my long search for a solution that reflected my wishes and gave me peace of mind, in 2010 I created a living trust, a legal document detailing what would happen to my possessions after my passing. Then I met with my daughters and sons for a celebratory lunch and gave each of them a copy of the trust. I also volunteered to answer their questions. I added a letter acknowledging the sentiment that their real inheritance was having each other and the love they shared, which was far greater than their many differences. I asked them to preserve their love all through the distribution process.

Creating a living trust was my way to be proactive in that matter. It was different from what my parents did, because I lived in the US and there were five instead of two heirs. Most likely the best solution for you and your family will be different too. The commonality of any inheritance decision is, after getting clear on your desires, share them with your loved ones. In doing that, it's possible to prevent misunderstanding and dysfunction in a highly emotional time at a family member's transition.

I don't mean to imply that being proactive by creating a legal document about how to apportion assets will resolve discord among families, but it helps open up a way to talk about the subject.

In some cases, however, you may need to have further conversations, making your reasoning clear to your heirs, even while you reserve the right to keep some details private.

This happened to me, and it allowed me to get crystal clear on my relationship with money and share that with my kids.

Nine years after that luncheon, early in 2019, one of my children disagreed with my decision not to disclose the current amount of money the other siblings owed me.

He took my decision as a lack of trust and felt hurt. He stopped calling me. I felt troubled and hurt by this, but I believed my decision was the best way to maintain family harmony. The agreements I made with each of the children were private. I missed his calls, when we had kept each other updated on our lives. I was sad and didn't see a resolution on the horizon.

After a couple weeks of reflection, I decided to share with my family my relationship with money and what it meant to me. I wrote a letter to all my children and their spouses with the hope they would understand where I was coming from.

Excerpts From the Letter

"Today I see money as a means to an end, something convenient, like oil that makes the life machine work smoother. For me, money never was, is, or will be an end. I don't want to be rich, and I feel thankful and blessed that the Universe always provides for me. By choice, I live a nice life that highly satisfies me without luxuries. I give to my favorite charities and support your financial needs when I can.

I enjoy making it easier for us to celebrate vacations together, covering some common expenses. Those celebrations, when the three generations of our family are together, are among my favorite things. Maybe everyone's.

"I use my personal criteria, maternal instincts, and deep desire to be an instrument of peace and harmony among us in the way I handle money matters. You don't have to agree with my decisions, just accept them, for I am the only one deciding about money and properties that belong exclusively to me.

"After my passing, when you receive your share, it will be your money, and only you will decide how to use it. That is your privilege and your responsibility.

"At the time of receiving our inheritance, I worked with Rosa Mari to execute our parents' oral and written desires in a deeply satisfying way for both of us, as we put our mutual love and their memory above the many details and decisions of the distribution.

"When your turn comes, my heart's desire is that the love you have for each other and my memory will guide you, too. I would like you to collaborate with Ignacio, my trustee, making it easier for him to complete his task. I wish for all of you to agree and be satisfied with the results.

"I want my inheritance to make your bond stronger, and I hope that following my trust directions will unite you even more. Can you all make this your intention, too? I hope you will follow the path of staying together and not allowing money and material things to separate you, as sadly happens to too many families."

Then I apologized for any harsh words I had used in the heat of some conversations, asking their forgiveness for my human frailties. And I concluded:

"My main purpose in life is to be an instrument of peace. It has given me happiness and fulfillment. May love, peace, and understanding prevail among the eight of you, my children and their spouses, as well as my grandchildren and all of my future descendants."

I sent the letter with a sense of solemnity, knowing it was part of my legacy as I bared my soul in a matter that was often controversial or unclear among families.

The letter was well received, with supportive answers sharing my intention to keep their bond strong after my passing, and even calling their siblings their biggest treasure. And the conflicted one returned to his weekly calls.

It is important to have our priorities clear when preventing or managing possible material conflicts.

Invitation

To prevent possible conflicts among your heirs, try this:

1. Give some time to collect your thoughts about what you would like to happen to your possessions after your passing.

2. Select and create a legal document that reflects them. Add a letter to your heirs that reflects your wishes for them to stay in harmony with each other and add any other important issue to you.

3. Give a copy of the document and letter to each of your heirs. Make yourself available to answer their questions.

If there is a misunderstanding with money or possessions, try this:

1. Discern what will be the best action to take to overcome it.

2. Clarify your position with money and material possessions, and express it clearly so they will understand it and eventually accept it, even if they disagree.

3. If needed, apologize for any harsh words or any other shortcomings in your interactions.

Money

To close this chapter that examines common obstacles on our journey of living a life of peace, I'd like to talk about money.

We touched on this a little in the section about inheritance within the greater goal of preserving family ties, and covered being proactive and managing misunderstandings related to money matters. But money plays a much greater role in our lives on a daily basis. It touches every part of our lives, often dictating where and in what circumstances we can live.

We know that money is an external *thing* in our life, but we also know it can cause us inner conflict.

Each person through their own life circumstances tends to develop their own way of relating to money. And, as with our relationships with people, the way we relate to it changes throughout our lives.

Our journey to inner peace with respect to money begins by asking ourselves: *How do I relate to money at this time in my life? Is it a source of distress or am I at ease, relaxed, and peaceful about it?*

If at this time in your life you feel peaceful in your relationship with money, nothing more is needed, but if you are not, this is an opportunity to look deeper. We will take a look at some scenarios and investigate the source of our distress and how it is connected to money.

There is no question that many of us are struggling with money now and are having difficulty making ends meet. Some of us have lost jobs, some have cumbersome credit card debts, medical bills, or student loans, and others of us are living beyond our means. We may feel anxious, afraid, or even desperate. We may get paranoid and overwhelmed and be unable to see a way out of debt. On top of all that, there is something like a silent agreement among most people not to talk about money or money issues. Getting into trouble with debt or not making enough money often has a shameful aspect to it, as if we intentionally put ourselves in this position. There is also the personal integrity part of it. If you end up in a position where you are not able to pay your obligations, you might feel a deep sense of failure. Whether you feel ashamed within yourself or because of how you look to others, it's important to take the time to investigate the disturbance.

When we feel ashamed we tend to clam up and "keep it to ourselves," perhaps because we are afraid of being criticized.

Holding our shame inside, however, does not bring us inner peace. I have found it quite liberating to break the cycle by talking openly about my money issues with select people. It's helpful to talk to people who can listen thoughtfully or people who have expertise. Talking about our money problems aloud with others can propel us to move on and begin to search for finding potential solutions to handle them. Sometimes, those people share ideas and a different and helpful approach to money. Seeing through another's eyes can be quite inspiring. We all know different people with similar socioeconomic situations, but one may seem to be at peace and feeling content, while another sees only lack. *Why?* Money itself is not causing the problem, but rather our attitude toward money. Being introduced to other people's attitudes and ideas about money and money issues can help us break through our own conditioning, which has contributed to our embarrassment or shame.

In my long life, I have gone through many different situations with money—from living frugally though happily as an immigrant child in Venezuela, to having more than enough to meet my needs as a working married woman, to going bankrupt as a single mom in the USA after a friend maxed out one of my credit cards.

The first two life circumstances were important because they served as a backdrop to my conditioning. I was raised to live frugally, and I was fine with it. Then, when I was working and living in Venezuela with my husband, our focus was not on accumulating more and more money and becoming rich, but rather on educating people. We both worked at the local university, making a moderate, though comfortable living and we were at ease with money. I believed at that point that money was not a problem if you lived frugally and responsibly and worked in an area meaningful to you. Thus, I was ill-prepared when money became a problem, and I discovered that alongside what seemed to be a helpful stand about money, I had adopted a set of values that I would use harshly against my own self when I got into trouble.

What I want to talk to you about is what happened during that bankruptcy because it was this event more than anything that forced me to decide how I was going to relate to money, even when I was in a situation of extreme debt that caused me great concern and unrest. In the context of this new disaster, I was put to the test: could I maintain my priority for peace, in spite of my significant financial challenges?

Let's take a look at what this looked like for me. Of course your own circumstances will be different, but if you are reading this book and have made it this far, it is because you, too, have a desire to make peace your highest priority.

Bankruptcy

It was 1999, and I had moved back to San Diego permanently. I was working hard and was successful in changing career paths, but struggled to pay my bills; I hadn't yet been able to turn my volunteer mediation practice into a paid job. This kind of money struggle was new for me. Then, suddenly, as I was working out how to earn more money, my already burdened financial obligations doubled as an arrangement I had with a friend went sideways.

My friend had turned to me for help because his credit was not good, so I lent him one of my credit cards. He and I had an agreement that he would make the monthly payments directly to the bank. Instead, he maxed out the credit card and stopped making the monthly payments. To my dismay, when I reached out to him, he never returned my calls, and disappeared from my life.

It was not only distressing to lose a friendship under these terms, but also financially devastating. At the time, I was struggling to pay my own bills, and then they doubled. It was impossible to assume his debt in addition to mine; I was already receiving threatening calls and notifications from debt collectors. I felt utterly defeated. Not knowing what to do, I searched for the advice of experts. To my surprise, a seasoned public financial advisor told me my best solution was to file for bankruptcy.

What? I asked incredulously.

Bankruptcy was not an avenue I had ever considered. In the past, I had paid my debts and worked hard as a responsible person. I wanted to continue doing that to keep my sense of integrity. I could not be a negligent person who was a burden to society.

Those first days after receiving the bankruptcy advice, I cried as if I would never stop, feeling the depths of human failure. In my mind, I had failed at two very important life issues I highly valued: first, my marriage, and now, my financial obligations.

As I sat in my living room at the depths of despair, a little voice inside gently reminded me that I had dedicated myself to living in peace. That little voice told me it was important to feel all these disturbing feelings, but reminded me not to dwell on them because it did not benefit me or resolve my situation.

I was at another crossroads. I could continue to beat myself up for having gotten in this predicament or stop and face the facts that were immediately before me: I was in irreconcilable debt. I needed to keep moving forward. I needed help. A possible solution had been presented to me by the senior financial advisor, a reliable source. All I needed was to keep myself open long enough to take the next step. Apprehensive and with my self-esteem at zero, I looked for a lawyer.

Much to my surprise, everything changed for me at the very first meeting, where the bankruptcy lawyer told me, "The law is giving you a second chance for a new financial beginning. There is nothing to be ashamed of."

His words surprised me and interrupted my own conditioning, eventually stopping my self-loathing for being in this situation. *A second chance? Wow. So, I would be a citizen in good standing after bankruptcy? What a relief.*

And there it was, the choice: I could stay stuck in my old way of thinking or adopt a new way that was kinder to myself and free myself of shame.

Then, because I valued peace above all else, I opened myself up to another way of thinking; I let his words change my perception about my situation. My lost sense of integrity returned. *Maybe I was not a "failure" after all. Maybe, I was choosing this last resort, a legal one, to put my finances in order and make it through a rough patch.*

Going through this with my eyes and heart open, being willing to feel the feelings as they arose, seeing my own conditioning and then redirecting my attention to living in peace, proved to be a fertile learning ground for life lessons that helped me rekindle peace within myself.

I also learned two valuable lessons, the first one: not lending a credit card to a friend. The second: to limit the use of credit cards to what I am able to repay in a month. Free from the burden of old debts, I was ready to live within my means, ending the story of creating debt. This simple common-sense formula brought me great results for my peace of mind.

Ultimately, instead of resenting myself for having to go through bankruptcy, I felt deep gratitude, especially to the United States, for giving me a second chance so I could learn new lessons without being persecuted.

Once the burden of my debt was gone and I forgave myself for my mistakes, I relaxed and regained my peace of mind, enriched by the lessons I learned.

Five years ago, I wrote an intention that prevails independent of whatever financial challenges exist in the moment or in the future for me. It has been liberating to adopt the following intention: *I ask divine guidance in all my financial decisions, so I can accomplish my one goal: to permanently experience inner peace with all the joy it brings.*

Steps to Take When Dealing With Difficult Money Issues:

1. Admit there is a problem.

2. Instead of hiding away, begin talking to others. Seek the help of those who will listen carefully. Seek the advice of experts in the field.

3. Allow yourself to feel whatever you are feeling and also pay attention to the stories in your head informing you about the issue.

4. Notice what your conditioning is around money issues.

5. Remember the stories are just your own conditioning, not absolute truth.

6. Show yourself compassion.

7. Open yourself to a different way of looking at the issue. What do other people think about the situation? How do others handle your situation?

8. Learn from your mistakes.

9. Forgive yourself.

10. Follow the guidance that feels the best for you after listening to experts and well-intentioned friends.

Invitation

1. Money issues are stressful. Take a deep breath and know you are not alone and there are ways to handle it.

2. Use your persistence to find the solution that fits best for you.

Part 4

Peace as a Journey

"Lord, make me an instrument of your peace.
Where there is hatred, let me sow love."
—Saint Francis of Assisi

So far, dear readers, we have been partaking in an inner journey to living in peace. First, we realized the most important place to start is to set an intention to live in peace. Then, we investigated how to orient our lives toward the qualities that are conducive to keep and enhance peace. These qualities include forgiveness, kindness, gratitude, respect, living in the moment, enthusiasm, and persistence. Then, we considered the obstacles that get in the way of keeping our intention to live in peace. We considered how inner conflicts, interpersonal disconnection, and external conflicts can present special challenges to living in peace and how we can overcome them.

Now we are going to spread our wings even more and investigate how to continue our journey of living in peace. When we do this, we will begin to recognize that each of us can be an instrument of peace, and we can begin to look for opportunities to spread peace in our daily life.

All along our journey, we keep learning. It is normal that sometimes we stumble or take a wrong turn. After noticing it and putting any self-judgment aside, we acknowledge our human frailties with compassion, forgive ourselves, and refocus on our peaceful journey. *A Course in Miracles* reminds us to "choose again," and graciously accept our mistakes. Some months ago and in spite of my already long journey, I stumbled when I harshly complained to a car rental employee. When I noticed my error, I apologized to him, forgave myself, and we returned to a friendly interaction. We are all human, we make mistakes, but we can correct our course once we recognize our mistake and show ourselves compassion.

Chapter 12

Making Friends

Being an instrument of peace doesn't need to be dramatic. It could come from a simple idea that pops into your mind about how to extend your inner contentment to your fellow humans. This happened to me some years ago. Living on the fourth floor of a building, I often ride the elevator with others. It always strikes me how people ignore each other in elevators, many times looking at the elevator floor or their phone screens, as though the only important thing is arriving at your destination and the time on the elevator is unimportant. I gave some thought to that common behavior. What came to me was that I wanted something different. I wanted to change the culture of strangers trapped in an elevator and connect with my neighbors, so I promised myself to speak to the other elevator passengers.

For many years now I might say, "Another beautiful day in San Diego!" or "Ready for work?" or "Taking your dog for a stroll?" or "What a beautiful smile your baby has!" Lo and behold, I got to know my neighbors. We have enjoyed many lively conversations and ended up wishing each other a good day or evening. Sometimes I witness the other passengers' moods improve. These simple conversations keep me in the moment and bring others back to the moment too. A win-win. "Strangers are friends you have not met yet." This phrase impacted me when I first heard it, and it is true. I cannot wait for the pandemic restrictions to be over, so I can ride with my neighbors in the elevator again.

One thing I have learned on my journey is that a person's name can be the sweetest word they hear. Once I discovered this, I began changing my interactions with people. I began to make a point of asking them for their name. For instance, when I go to a restaurant, I ask the name of my server at the first opportunity, and then I use it. This makes our interaction more personal. When I leave, I thank them by name. I have found this to be remarkably simple and effective. It makes me feel good, and it seems to make them feel better too. I notice their demeanor is more relaxed and usually they smile.

Prior to my awakening in 1978, and even though I was a successful woman according to society's standards, deep inside I was unhappy. This propelled me on my journey of self-discovery to find out that working in the field of economics was not my calling and was part of the reason I felt unfulfilled. Then, I discovered working and interacting with other people interested in improving and striving to live their best lives attracted me, and working with these people gave meaning to my work. So, I began the arduous though heart-propelled task of changing careers. Along the way, I discovered that inner satisfaction comes from pursuing what is truly meaningful to me, not what my culture taught me and not from the opinions of my peers. This gave me the inner strength to align my life toward bringing peace to myself and others and ultimately brought me the elusive happiness I so craved.

Living in a space of lasting peace means we have chosen peace as our highest aspiration, and when faced with any disturbance, whether internal or external, we do whatever it takes to return to inner peace and contentment.

I fell down many times along the way. I fought negative inner voices that told me I couldn't or I shouldn't, yet I persisted and learned that practice and compassion are integral to maintaining inner peace. The more we practice, the easier it becomes. Always keep in mind, if we can begin with "a little willingness," then we will be guided to find solutions to disturbances.

For me that willingness came at the beginning of my journey when I was stuck blaming my ex for my unhappiness. From my reading in *A Course in Miracles,* I knew I needed to forgive him to find peace within myself.

A Course encourages us to see everyone, including those we are unable to forgive, as innocent. At first, that seemed impossible to me. But, I had begun to realize that my way of dealing with the suffering and challenges of life was not working. I started slowly—with "a little willingness"—to try to see his infidelity as something he just *did,* not something he did specifically to inflict pain on me. This paved the way for me to forgive him and also forgive myself for things I had done that unintentionally hurt others, like forgetting important dates like birthdays or other celebrations.

Accepting total responsibility for myself and my happiness and letting go of victimhood was the next step on my journey.

After seven transformative years (1978 to 1985) of working on my fundamental life issues, I found a new and real me born from my conditioned past. Dear reader, take heart: those seven years, while sometimes difficult, were not long and arduous; they were enlivening and uplifting because I began to feel happier inside myself, which propelled me and gave me hope for a different way of living. As the moments of peace became more and more frequent, I got clear on choosing peace as my highest priority and began to learn how to return to inner peace when I stumbled. I am humbled by what those years showed me and grateful for the attitude of living that I learned then, which I have now enjoyed for over thirty-five years.

As that new and authentic person rose inside, I adopted a set of values and beliefs based upon my own findings to replace the unexamined values I had learned in my childhood and youth. This new set of values has been the guiding force of my life ever since. I continue enhancing and refining them, adapting them to new situations that arise. We all can do that, independent of our age. I began at forty-one, and I have been abundantly rewarded. You, dear reader, can begin now, whatever age you are.

Invitation

1. I invite you to reach out to others you are in contact with—neighbors, strangers, or homeless people you see. A simple smile or a "good morning" can improve someone's day. Your inclusive attitude is needed in the world.

2. On our journey to peace it is important to pay attention to what brings ourselves and others ease and contentment. This can be noticing simple things, like learning the name of your server, or it can be examining the deeper issues in our life that are causing us unrest.

Chapter 13

Happiness, Joy, and Peace

Human evolution is about accepting our life as a journey of self-discovery, one where we revise and discard old habits and conditioning which chain us to self-limiting beliefs and repeating ancestral patterns. No matter one's age, there is always more to discover and actualize. This is an exciting realization: *The more we live, the more we can become the best version of ourselves.* We can continuously evolve; we only need to be open and keep choosing it.

I learned this again recently while having my son Pascual, who is now in his fifties, living with me for the last year and a half. Before moving in, Pascual and I had not spent significant time together for over thirty years, except for family vacations. He had been busy with his career that included lots of traveling, and lived in Venezuela for some years. He moved back to the United States to focus on his health and personal growth and stayed with me in the transitional period.

I knew him and loved him from our time together when he was growing up, and though I have always missed having him close to me, I knew my memories of him as a child could affect my impression of the man he had become after so many years. I didn't want my preconceived notions to color our interactions in ways that could be detrimental to our relationship in the present moment, so I decided to step outside of what I knew of him as a child and get to know him again. I intentionally adopted a fresh, curious attitude toward him. Instead of clinging to the past, I chose to live in the present so we could get reacquainted.

What happened was quite rewarding. I discovered many traits he had adopted as an adult, like tidiness and cleanliness, his delicious cooking while humming, his availability to grocery shop and run other errands, and his willingness to do home repairs. His cheerful demeanor in our daily interactions became a wonderful addition to my life, especially since it coincided with the confinement of the global COVID-19 pandemic. Assessing our life together today, I can see that our understanding, acceptance, and enjoyment of each other continues to flourish. He has helped me live in the moment, keeping me growing and evolving.

Being on our journey to peace can support us in our evolution. As we evolve, we have a continual opportunity to examine our own doubts. We are not always convinced that happiness is possible or that we deserve to be happy, as we discussed in Chapter 9. In fact, sometimes we even sabotage our happiness by clinging to old beliefs. With my son Pascual, I intentionally let go of my ideas of who he was as a child so I could learn who he is now, thirty years later.

Initiating my own journey at forty-one, it took me a while to accept and understand that each of us has an innate right to be happy, and we can either assist or hinder ourselves in getting there. My own awakening to my innate right to be happy and the role I had in sustaining it came forty years ago. As a brand-new student of *A Course in Miracles*, I was surprised to read in Lesson 100:

"God's will for me is perfect happiness. And why should I choose to go against his will?"

The lesson continues: "Without your joy, His joy is incomplete. Without your smile, the world cannot be saved. While you are sad, the light that God Himself appointed as the means to save the world is dim and lusterless, and no one laughs because all laughter can but echo yours."

This notion that God (or the Universe or a higher power) *wants* me to be perfectly happy contradicted my old belief system that saw all human beings as sinners condemned to suffering. The claim from *A Course* appealed to me and resonated as truth in my heart. I decided to adopt it. And you, dear reader, can adopt it too.

Many other spiritual traditions from all over the world affirm that happiness is not only possible but it is our birthright to experience now.

A Buddhist prayer reads, "May all beings everywhere be happy and free."

Don Miguel Ruiz, in his book on Toltec wisdom, *The Four Agreements,* invites us "to change the dream we are living from fear and drama to love and joy."

Even the American Declaration of Independence in 1776 establishes that, in addition to life and liberty, the pursuit of happiness is a right we all have.

Everywhere and at all times, the voices of wisdom acknowledge our right to be happy, joyful, peaceful, and free now.

Happiness and peace come hand in hand. Happiness is a conscious decision. Events are just that: events; they are neutral. To experience happiness as a constant in our life, we can be open to accept life experiences as they show up without labeling them as good or bad. We get to decide what to do with our experiences. Are we going to be happy or unhappy in the presence of life's unpredictable events? Perhaps we need to change our perspectives and see them from another angle. Maybe we need to go deeper to find the hidden benefits of a challenging situation.

Embracing our life experiences exactly as they are presented is the key to continued happiness. When facing challenges, instead of accepting the tendency to close down, I invite you and all of us to keep our hearts and minds open, with a curious attitude ready to meet and resolve any situation to extend our precious happiness. It was helpful to adopt this curious attitude during Pascual's stay with me and allowed me to discover and enjoy the man he had become.

With an open mind, we have the ability to remain enthused, challenged, and inspired throughout this journey called life. It is our choice. Happiness, as well as peace, is an inside job, and it is available to whoever chooses that path. We are all invited to join the happy campers' society. We all get to decide how to experience life.

Benefits

In the face of great challenges, it can feel almost impossible to *choose* happiness. I am not pointing to the instant gratification of eating an ice cream kind of happiness, but rather a much deeper flavor of happiness that we *can* choose. This comes from living an authentic life aligned with our heartfelt desires, in which we actively do our best and forgive ourselves quickly when we fail. This form of happiness manifests as a calm inner contentment. It's worth everything to pursue this kind of happiness. So, let's investigate some of the benefits of choosing happiness, as peace.

When we choose the peaceful way, we are adding elements to our fulfillment that grow as we move along. As we begin to examine our lives, unlearning our conditioning and exploring values that resound in us, we begin to breathe in the air of an authentic life, one in alignment with our chosen heartfelt beliefs where we are 100 percent accountable for our own happiness, instead of being victims of our conditioning and repeating ancestral patterns ingrained in us. This is the basis of enjoying our journey.

When my journey began, I needed to overcome my strong habit of blaming others for my unhappiness or shortcomings, walk away from victimhood, and accept total responsibility for my life and happiness. Most of the time, we are not able to change what is happening in the world, but we always can change our perspective on our circumstances. That is how powerful we all are. It begins with acceptance of what is.

In Chapter 3 on Unleashing Happiness, we spoke about a common tendency to delay our happiness. Whether you feel unworthy, or want to blend with unhappy people, no matter what your "reason" is, I invite you first to see and accept your resistance and then move to resolve it and accept your destiny to become a joyful, peaceful person who brings happiness to others. When you are ready, you can try it. There is only one thing to lose: suffering. Does this appeal to you?

Below is a checklist for happiness. Take a look and, with a curious attitude, enjoy this journey of examining your own life, routing out the areas that bring you suffering, and finding other ways of moving forward.

Invitation

1. I invite you to see events in your life as neutral instead of labeling them as good or bad. When we encounter life's challenges with an open mind, we naturally focus on finding solutions instead of problems.

2. I invite you to unlearn old conditioning that may have been a part of your life for years. We can retrain our minds.

3. I invite you to consider changing the way you spend your time, for example, spend less time focusing on what is wrong, like watching news, and more time on uplifting activities, like following your heart, going for walks, and enjoying your loved ones.

4. I invite you to focus on gratitude and move away from "what we don't have" in our lives and toward "what we do have." Writing in a gratitude journal is an excellent way to find and focus on reasons to be grateful.

5. I invite you to consistently apply the thought that whatever we focus on grows.

6. I invite you to ask the question—what is the most important thing to me right now? How can I nurture that so it can grow?

Chapter 14

Natural Teachers

One final comment on expanding our happiness, joy, and peace as we go through life: look for your natural teachers. Today, at eighty-five, I see my life as an adventure in discovering more about myself all the time, and I declare this will continue until my last breath. I invite you to join me and see life as a school where we are all students.

Sometimes, we underestimate the powerful influence of those to whom we are closest. Maybe we consider our personality or our outlook on life to be too different or our age difference too great. Look again, dear readers. The people closest to us are likely to reflect an aspect of ourselves we may be reluctant to see. These people are not necessarily family, although they are for me; they may also be neighbors, coworkers, or good friends.

In my early forties, I began to notice that my children were teaching me lessons I needed to learn, not necessarily lessons I *wanted* to learn. But the nature of a good teacher is that they teach us what is important, not what we want or what is easy. When people ask me how many children I have,

I answer: "Five, they are my five teachers. I am lucky that the Universe sent me not one or two, but five teachers."

Our teachers can be our mirrors reflecting ourselves, and sometimes we don't appreciate seeing our true reflection. It can be shocking when we are first introduced to a new life lesson. Today, my kids and their families, including my grandkids, are my constant teachers, and eventually, I cherish what I learn from them and accept their gifts to keep me improving and evolving.

For instance, from my daughter Verónica, I have learned flexibility. Often when we make a plan, she will make a change or two. She always gives me enough notice and sweetly explains why, and it usually makes sense. But at first, I resisted the changes. It takes me a moment to remember: Verónica is a mirror reflecting my rigidity. This is not a trait I want to see in myself, but I am grateful she shows me. Once I see my rigidity, I acknowledge it and show myself compassion, then relax and accept the change.

Here is an important lesson I learned from my youngest grandchild, ten-year-old Joaquín: "Talent" can be applied to many things besides scholarly accomplishments, which is how I tended to apply it. Joaquín is a natural born actor and singer and has been performing since the age of seven, when he played Bert in a children's version of *Mary Poppins*. He has expanded my narrow vision of talent to include artists and their unique approach to life.

Accepting our closest people as our teachers can be quite rewarding for all of us. I invite each of us to open our hearts to our natural teachers and learn from them. No doubt, they will expand our horizons, increase our inclusivity, and allow us to enjoy people and their gifts at a deeper level.

This exercise keeps us humble and in the learning mode so we can rise to the occasion to become better versions of ourselves. There is always room for improvement. If we are alive, we are not done.

When I turned eighty, I declared it was my decade of joy. I wrote an intention that I read daily, stating joy and peace as the essence of my being. As I mentioned in Chapter 11, soon after the coronavirus pandemic began, I found I could transform my initial perception about it as a terrible thing that life was inflicting upon us. After we acknowledge that it has upended life as we know it and killed millions of people around the world, we can ask ourselves, is there a silver lining amidst the tragedy and chaos? What about if our life during the pandemic has been good? We could choose to see the Universe as providing extra time to advance something we care about that we hadn't made time to pursue in our busy life before. And for me, I was able to dedicate the extra time at home to finish writing this book. As a consequence, I am following my bliss while staying safe and healthy in confinement. You too can do this, dear reader. You can always access joy in your journey, as you certainly deserve.

Invitation

1. Consider who in your life has taught you the most. Were these lessons always easy? Probably not, but usually they are important for our evolution.

2. What experiences in your life have taught you the most? Sometimes our most painful lessons bring us the most insight and humility.

Chapter 15
Bonus Tips

N ow that we have gone together on an investigation into the qualities and potential pitfalls of living a peaceful life, and have tasted the potential for living in peace and spreading peace wherever we go, I want to leave you with a few special tips that helped my journey of peace and may help yours too. These include letting go of being in a hurry, finding humor, and looking for your favorite things.

Being in a Hurry

"Hurry up" or "Apúrate, date prisa," are demands on myself I have had to work hard to erase from my inner dialogue. They were so ingrained in me, intruding on my thoughts as I advanced a project, enjoyed my family, or prepared to go out. When I started paying attention to my inner dialogue, I began to notice that the "hurry up" voice was robbing the natural joy from my activities and making me feel anxious, far away from being at peace. As my son-in-law Andrés once said, hurriedness takes away the quality of life, as we are no longer present in the moment but anxious to complete the task at hand.

To be able to eliminate that inner dialogue, I needed to find out where it came from. *Why am I so often in a hurry?* One thing I noticed was my tendency to procrastinate and leave things to the last minute. This contributed to a sense of panic and activated the demanding voice inside of me: *Hurry up, Nere, you are late.*

Unlearning the bad habit of leaving things to the last minute took time. I failed many times and discovered I needed to stop beating myself up about it and begin practicing deep self-compassion, forgiving myself for the innumerable times I broke the pact. This allowed me to keep practicing. When I advanced in the process, I knew my next step was to tell my friends and loved ones about my decision so they would know and maybe support me in succeeding.

One day, I was getting ready to go to the movies with my family. One of my kids came to me with an impatient demeanor: "Hurry up, Mom, we are late." I stopped what I was doing, calmly looked into her eyes, and said: "I need ten more minutes. If you cannot wait, it's fine, go ahead without me." This was a powerful statement to myself. I felt I was breaking a tacit agreement to hurry each other. Certainly, I didn't need external reinforcement about something I was working to overcome. It became clear to me then—I would no longer accept or offer external invitations to hurry up. My peace of mind is more important. If people around you aren't supporting your decision to let go of your stressful tendency to rush yourself, it is always helpful to remind them where you stand.

Javier, my dear first cousin who was like a big brother to me, was also instrumental in reinforcing my decision to overcome my drive to be in a hurry. Besides being a successful architect, Javier was a wise, calm man with a big heart.

In our many lively conversations when I visited Venezuela twenty years ago, he would often say, "Nere, I never am in a hurry." It was my experience of him, always calm and present, taking the needed actions without being pushed or stressed out.

I admired that about Javier. He inspired me to stop my hurriedness, remain calm, and move from my center. Eventually, I wanted to erase hurriedness, both from my life and from my vocabulary.

Recently, a situation tested me on how I was doing with hurriedness. A month before the time we thought the writing for this book would be complete, I talked to my coach about the timeline and she felt I needed some extra time. Even though completing my book has been a priority for me for a while, I accepted her expertise without fighting, reminding myself I didn't need to rush the process, but instead, take the time necessary to feel satisfied with the final result. And I keep working to make it possible. It seems we can treat time the same as we treat money: "Time exists to serve me, not me to serve time."

Invitation

1. If you find yourself often in a hurry, first acknowledge it.
2. Ask yourself what changes you might need to make to eradicate it.
3. Be diligent with work- or school-related projects that have a time limit. Plan how you will cover and complete each phase. Avoid leaving it to the last minute.
4. Tell people around you that you are working on eliminating the feeling of being rushed, so they can support you or at least know where you are.

About Humor

The more I live, the more I value humor. Humor can give a twist to something we are going through personally or in a relationship by taking away the sting of a situation. No wonder it has been said that *laughter is the best medicine.* And I add, *with the side effect of making everybody more relaxed and joyful.* Do not confuse humor with sarcasm, however, which can be hurtful to others. There is a difference between joking *about* others that can be critical and joking *with* others that usually is warm and welcome.

My third son, Pascual, who shares my living space, has a good sense of humor that I believe has ignited my own. A tall man, he graciously reaches high things in the kitchen cabinets at my request, while I laugh about how short I am. Together we have enjoyed laughing about our idiosyncrasies. Humor has spiced up our time together.

I found a great subject for my jokes is myself. For example, I have an accent. I learned to accept it and decided not to use my time and energy to get rid of it. Interestingly, because I come originally from the Basque Country, I have an accent in both my adopted countries, in both English and Spanish. I jokingly ask myself *Am I always giving a hint to the listener that this is not my first language?* Perhaps, next time I meet someone, and they ask me where I'm from I'll reply, "Born and raised in Southern California, can't you tell from my accent, dude?" Laughing about my mistakes and imperfections helps me to relax and accept my perceived flaws. And you, dear reader, can joke about your traits too.

Invitation

Is there anything from your youth that was very serious, but when you reflect on it now, seems funny? Remember that with perspective, humor can avail itself to even your biggest concerns, so try to adopt it as early as possible to bring a light spirit to your heart.

Favorite Things

On our journey of peace, we want to pay attention to what naturally attracts us and makes us happy. Joseph Campbell coined this idea long ago: *Follow your bliss.* I would add this: Pay attention to what enlivens your senses. When we actively pay attention to our senses, we are in the present, experiencing the moment, and as I have said before, this moment is all we have. This moment is where peace resides.

If you are drawn to the outdoors, you may want to take up hiking, noticing the trees and birds, feeling the ground beneath your feet, smelling the earthly delights. Or maybe you are drawn to spending time in the water swimming or surfing, feeling the rush of water against your skin, or simply laying on the beach, feeling the rays of sun upon your skin. Or maybe you discover you love the feel of wet clay in your hands and take up pottery, or that you love cooking, enlivening your sense of smell and taste, creating new delectables.

Following our sensual attractions and making them part of our normal activities makes our journey more joyful. And when we are joyful, we are naturally at peace. I invite you to explore these activities. They can become hobbies, or they can be so dominant that you decide to make them your life's work. However it unfolds, following your inclination and enlivening your senses is one of life's greatest natural gifts that can contribute deeply to living a peaceful, fulfilling life.

My inclination was music. My music never rose to the level of a career, but it has brought me much joy in my life. At eight years old, already living in Venezuela, I was selected to be part of my school choir, where, as an alto, I learned to harmonize, a breathtaking experience that made me vibrate inside. That first choir experience fed my immense attraction to all kinds of music, which has continued to give me pleasure to this day.

This summer, on our family vacation, we had the chance to sing and dance to the rhythm of well-known songs played by a band. It was one of my favorite moments of our vacation. The memories of singing and dancing together continue to give me abundant joy.

Singing and harmonizing were also important parts of my Basque culture, where it was understood that everyone could sing as long as they could talk. I also attended a public conservatory that gave me an appreciation for classical music and deepened my interest in harmonizing in choirs. I participated in many choirs in Venezuela, singing in Spanish and Basque.

Fast forward to my early seventies, when I was already living permanently in San Diego. I was invited to sing with the emerging Threshold Choir, committed to "Singing at the bedside of those at the threshold of life, bringing them ease, comfort, and presence." With my long love for choir singing and the appreciation for the amazing purpose of this choir, I joined this group of kind, calm, mature women. It was an unforgettable privilege to sing and offer soothing company to people in the sublime time of their transition and comfort their families and caregivers.

That was my last choir participation and first in an English-speaking one. I have been fortunate to sing in choirs in Basque, Spanish, and English, representing the three cultures that have shaped the person I am today.

At the present moment, I keep vibrating and get inspired listening to Beethoven's Ninth Symphony finale, the Ode to Joy, the inviting hymn to joy and hope for the whole of humanity, and to the accords of Handel's Alleluia.

Each of us has specific inclinations that we can find and dive into. Maybe you already know what those are for you, maybe you don't. Certainly, you can discover them and add enjoyment to your peaceful journey.

Inner peace is my main goal in life: constantly experiencing it within myself, no matter what is going on in the world or in my personal life. Every other goal comes after that and is always dependent on preserving my inner peace. The state of being peaceful can be obtained through changing our perception, going away from conflicts, and making peace with oneself, the Universe and others, personally and collectively.

I love the proverb "The highest happiness is peace." It is also my highest desire for you, dear reader: "May we all be at peace." Like these words from *A Course*, "The peace of God is my one goal, the aim of my living here, the end I seek, my purpose and my function and my life."

Invitation

1. Pay attention to your natural inclinations and make a concerted effort to explore them.

2. Observe how your life enjoyment increases when you spend time doing what you love.

Chapter 16

Surrender and Transcendence

"Sweet, sweet surrender, live, live without care.
Like a fish in the water, like a bird in the air."

—JOHN DENVER

Once we embark on our path to live in peace, we discover that instead of making life a big drama, we can relax and surrender to what is before us. We respond to life instead of reacting. This results in peace, contentment, and joy and is a lesson we can draw on again and again, no matter how long we have been on the path.

The story that follows happened to me recently. Using many of the tricks I learned on my long journey to retrain my mind to live in peace, I was able to change an experience that is usually frightening into a pleasant one, one that I am grateful I went through. When we choose the peaceful path, changing the way we think and act, we all have the capacity to transform our experiences from fearful to loving and hopeful. It's a matter of practicing our chosen way of thinking and applying it to the situations we face. Let us walk through this together.

On September 15, 2020, I received a phone call to set an appointment for a medical procedure my cardiologist recommended, to install a device called Watchman in my heart to prevent blood clots going to my brain that may cause another stroke. The proposed day was the following Monday. I looked into my calendar to discover that day, September 21st, was the United Nations International Day of Peace. Surprised and thrilled with the synchronicity, I accepted the appointment. I took it as a confirmation that the Universe selected that meaningful day to let me know that everything was in perfect order, and there was nothing to be concerned about; I was totally covered. I felt calm and looked forward to the procedure and the health benefits the device would provide.

This happened in the middle of the pandemic. But instead of panicking about all the possible unknowns, I relied on my highest intention to live in peace and again drew strength and purpose from this saying from *A Course in Miracles:*

"If I'm looking for the positive, I won't notice the negative. If I'm looking for the negative, I won't notice the positive. The vision of one world will cost you the vision of the other."

I focused on the fact that the pandemic had arrived in San Diego six months earlier, and the medical system already had made the changes needed to continue operating safely, as I had already experienced firsthand on my medical visits. I learned their new guideline that I needed to be alone to enter the facility.

To surrender is to stop fighting and instead, yield to a greater power, to our higher, real self, away from fear and negative projections, stopping anxious inner *what ifs*. We don't need to know and understand all the details of every situation we face, we must trust, relax, and allow ourselves to realize that all is well. Surrender is giving up control.

That doesn't mean to give up what we need to do to remain calm and at ease throughout the process. Be diligent, ask questions to get clear, and be well prepared; I even made a request to give myself extra peace of mind: to stay overnight at the hospital under the care of their trained personnel.

Then, I surrendered, accepting that a higher power was in charge and everything would be fine. I felt calm before the procedure. In other words, I did my best and then, I expected the best. And while I could not know the outcome, I could rest in peace that I had adequately prepared myself, and I was ready to receive the gifts of the experience, instead of resisting and fighting.

"It is what it is" is a phrase I hear often. Phrases like this are clear invitations to surrender. What happens in the world is what happens without our permission; screaming and fighting won't change things. These actions only serve to make us anxious and defensive, the opposite of peaceful.

What I experienced during my one day and night at the hospital was kindness and compassion, from the registration process to the end, when a nurse helped me into my daughter Nere's car. The personnel went beyond their duties to give me comfort and ease.

As I waited for my surgery, I could hear the jovial conversation and laughter of the nurses, an invitation to relax. The surgery suite was calming, too. Before I knew it, I was back in my space, with no memory of my procedure or prior intubation. I slept well, and in the morning, I woke up to a lovely view from my seventh-floor room where I gratefully went through my spiritual readings and had coffee and breakfast. What I most valued from my time at the hospital was the loving care I received. Staying overnight was a good decision, giving me the space to feel covered in my sleep and get ready to return home.

I emphasize the importance of looking for the positive in every situation, even the most challenging ones. Repeatedly, it has been said by many thinkers, including Oprah Winfrey: "What you focus on expands, and when you focus on the goodness in your life, you create more of it."

Staying present and open and not entertaining the possibility of complications has kept me free from fear. As *A Course in Miracles* teaches, my focus was on everything that went well and pleased me. As a consequence, my experience was one of joy and gratitude for all the care and kindness received.

Faith and trust are essential to surrender: Faith that you are giving in to something bigger than yourself and without human limitations, and trust that everything is in perfect order.

Every morning I read the last lessons of *A Course in Miracles,* a declaration to surrender the day to Spirit: "This holy instant I would give to you. Be you in charge. For I would follow you, certain that your directions give me peace."

We all can feel joy while going through a medical procedure or any other situation that is not necessarily pleasant or fun.

A big part of surrender has to do with accepting what is happening, looking for the positive, and focusing on what we want to grow, as we have been talking about; this is important to remember not just during larger life challenges but in day-to-day interactions as well. While we are learning, it is *normal* to stumble and look at the negative. But our goal as students of peace is to notice when we have begun looking at the negative, and with self-compassion, refocus again on the positive. *A Course in Miracles* acknowledges our human frailties and keeps repeating "choose again," to guide us to graciously accept our mistakes and move forward.

Today, after living in peace for over forty years, my human frailties still show sometimes, though less often. When they do, I rely on my practices to readjust my thinking, words, and actions. I choose again. This is another form of surrender. We let go of a position that we have held that contributes to distress instead of peace.

While having dinner one night this summer during our annual family vacation, my sweet daughter Verónica made a suggestion to all of us, and I responded to it in a rough, unkind way. Later that day, realizing my words were hurtful, I apologized to her. The next day, when the fourteen of us got together for dinner, I apologized again, as I felt she deserved to receive the apology in front of everyone, kids and grandkids who had witnessed my harsh words the night before. I have learned that the faster a sincere apology comes, the better. I encourage you to overcome any hesitancy you might have to apologize and do so as soon as possible to allow the return to a loving, peaceful understanding between yourself and others.

As children learning to walk, it is natural to stumble, and like them we can stand up, dust ourselves off, and continue trying until we learn the new skill. This practice is simple, but it takes time to learn. Retraining our mind to focus on the goodness in our life is a simple way to open the door to abundance, and it's available to you and me, to everyone, right now.

Invitation

When dealing with a crisis:

1. Accept what is happening.
2. Stop fighting and resisting.
3. Expect the best.
4. Be open and look for the benefits the situation can bring.
5. Stay present. Avoid anticipating possible future problems.
6. Be diligent. Ask questions to be well informed. Also ask for your needs or wants to be met.
7. When your own human frailty rises, forgive yourself and choose again.
8. When necessary, apologize.

Transcendence

Once we are committed to living in peace, we evolve into becoming an instrument of peace. It is the natural consequence.

As *A Course in Miracles* says, we teach what we want to learn, and at our core, what we most want to learn is to live in a quiet, undisturbed state of peace. We teach this not only with words but with our presence, thoughts, gestures, actions, and laughter. We exude peace. Being and living peacefully is our most important contribution to the evolution of humankind, and what we receive in return is what we most appreciate: expanded peace.

It is possible for humanity to enjoy the big win for all and live together in a world where everyone is accepted as a unique person who brings their special gift to the rest, where everyone can engage in their favorite role in harmony... "each group simply enjoying their Sunday at the park in their own way." Simple and powerful.

I invite you to begin or continue your peaceful journey, have fun on the ride, and know that with your journey, you are contributing toward a culture of peace for future generations to enjoy.

At the beginning of the millennium, the United Nations, in conjunction with many Peace Prize Nobel recipients, declared 2000 as the "International Year for a Culture of Peace."

"A Culture of Peace," as the UN defines, "is a set of values, attitudes, modes of behavior, and ways of life that reject violence and conflicts by tackling their root causes to solve problems through dialogue and negotiation among individuals, groups, and nations."

We all can contribute to creating a culture of peace with an inviting and inclusive attitude in our interactions throughout the day: taking children to school, going to work, cooking, cleaning for the family, or going for a stroll. Performing routine and ordinary tasks in an extraordinary way by staying in the moment and paying attention to whatever we are doing is a gift to the world. As in the example of riding the elevator, our reward is the deep satisfaction that the ordinary task can bring. The extra reward is knowing we are making a contribution to humanity evolving into a culture of peace, a direction that will benefit all.

St. Francis Prayer

Lord, make me an instrument of your peace;
Where there is hatred, let me sow love,
Where there is injury, pardon;
Where there is doubt, faith;
Where there is despair, hope;
Where there is darkness, light;
And where there is sadness, joy.

O Divine Master,
Grant that I may not so much seek
To be consoled as to console;
To be be understood as to understand;
To be loved as to love.
For it is in giving that we receive;
Is is in pardoning that we are pardoned;
And it is in dying that we are born to eternal life.

Before I leave you, dear reader, I have one last gift to share: The St. Francis Prayer. I have taken many pages to share with you a path to peace. But I am not the first to discover this way of being. The St. Francis Prayer says it all quite succinctly, and I invite you to make a copy and keep it close to you. This beautiful prayer has a way of surfacing just when it is most needed.

Like the Buddha, St. Francis was born to a very rich family, and as a child, received all kinds of material things. Nevertheless, he felt unfulfilled and renounced the lavish life to embark on a simple, austere path where he found his real self, and in so doing, became an example for us, many, many centuries later. He exemplifies that the external world is not the cause of our happiness or lack of it; finding and following our authentic self and serving others with our special gifts will give us all the peace and inner joy to manifest as happiness in our lives.

The Prayer of St. Francis is a clear guide on how to walk and interact through life. The first part of the prayer indicates how we can help others in different situations, while the second part invites us to give others what we want to receive— to be consoled, understood, and loved. The end reminds us how crucial it is to give abundantly, and in doing so, we will receive abundantly, like two sides of a coin.

The prayer reminds us we have company on our journey and shows us how to interact with people in our daily encounters, being there with them in their time of need. It is a simple and effective way to become an instrument of peace.

Because peace as a journey can be a simple choice does not imply it is an easy one. Like any journey, we encounter obstacles and make mistakes; it is part of being human. But we have what it takes to overcome the obstacles, accept our mistakes, forgive ourselves, and continue walking our chosen path.

If you have the question: Is it possible to stay in abiding peace?

The answer is yes, it is absolutely possible to live in abiding peace as your permanent state of being. I have lived that way for more than forty years, the last half of my life. It has allowed me to enjoy myself, and it becomes easier and easier as we practice the tools and discover new ones on our journey.

As I said earlier, The St. Francis Prayer has a way of showing up when it is most needed. It has touched my heart personally, too.

After my mom passed, and almost twenty years later after my dad passed, I was going through some of my dad's paperwork at his old home office in Caracas. I was surprised to find several copies of the very same prayer of peace I had been reciting daily. I cried holding the Spanish version of St. Francis' peace prayer personally typed by my father. Knowing I was continuing his legacy gave my practice a deeper meaning.

Inspired, I made copies of Dad's peace prayer, giving them to all his descendants. I envision this simple yet powerful prayer will also be meaningful and inspiring for my grandkids and later generations, as it has inspired me and many generations before us. And, my dear reader, I envision you inspired, too, while pursuing your peaceful journey.

Invitation

I invite you, dear reader, to live in peace for the rest of your days and feel assured that it is the best way to live, for you and for all of humanity.

"Let there be peace on earth, and let it begin with me."
—JILL JACKSON-MILLER AND SY MILLER

Did you enjoy the book?
Let friends and family
know.
Thankful,
Nere B

Acknowledgments

To my friend Dina and daughter Verónica for the inspirational conversations that made me decide to write this book.

To Verónica, my steady company throughout the four years of my writing journey, always offering supportive ideas and great enthusiasm.

To Lois Sunrich, editor of my first draft who lovingly and clearly directed me to find a writing coach, after my dissatisfaction with the first draft.

To Marni Freedman, for content editing the first draft and then becoming my writing coach for the next three years. She helped me to see what was relevant in my story, and refined several times until it became my legacy, the book I want to be remembered for. She was right there with me, offering encouraging support when, more than once, I was ready to quit. Wisely, she directed me to the many great collaborators in my writing adventure.

To Lindsey Salatka who patiently edited the subsequent versions, until the end. Her expertise is highly appreciated, including her eye to catch repetitions.

To Marijke McCandles, for helping the transition from a memoir to a self-help book, focusing on making the lessons

I learned useful to be applied by my reader, and giving an invitational tone.

To Valeria, my computer-savvy granddaughter, for being there when I needed simple and more complex technical support, with her big smile and natural ability to teach.

To Nené, best friend of my daughter Nere, for letting me know that she was eagerly waiting to read my book in a moment when I had decided to quit.

To my son Ignacio for being there all along the way, providing his special skills and loving support.

To my family and friends, you know who you are, who were there for me at different times and in different ways, kindly giving me encouragement and support, making it easier to complete my book.

About the Author

Nere Lartitegui, PhD., is a psychologist, counselor, conflict resolution mediator, peace advocate, and student of life. She is a blend of the Basque Country, Venezuela, and the United States, three cultures that influenced the person she is today.

Now eighty-five, Nere considers *The Missing Peace* her legacy and hopes to convey to her readers how to live a happy, fulfilled life with peace as a priority. She resides in San Diego, California.

Visit her at themissingpeacebook.net.

Made in the USA
Monee, IL
03 May 2024

57809772R00132